Termcap & Terminfo

Termcap & Terminfo

John Strang, Linda Mui, and Tim O'Reilly

O'REILLY®

Beijing · Cambridge · Köln · Paris · Sebastopol · Taipei · Tokyo

Termcap & Terminfo
by John Strang, Linda Mui, and Tim O'Reilly

Editor: Tim O'Reilly

Printing History:

1985:	First edition written by John Strang.
1986:	Second edition with minor corrections. Appendix A augmented by Dale Dougherty.
August 1987:	Minor revisions, index added. Revised page design by Linda Lamb and Dale Dougherty.
April 1988:	Third edition with major expansions by John Strang, Linda Mui, and Tim O'Reilly to include *terminfo* and update *termcap* to BSD 4.3 standard.
February 1989:	Additional review comments incorporated by Linda Mui.
September 1990:	Minor corrections.
April 1991:	Minor corrections.
July 1992:	Minor corrections.

This book is printed on acid-free paper with 85% recycled content, 15% post-consumer waste. O'Reilly & Associates is committed to using paper with the highest recycled content available consistent with high quality.

ISBN: 0-937175-22-6 [1/99]

TABLE OF CONTENTS

Page

Preface

Part 1: Tutorial

Chapter 1 Introduction

Chapter 2 Reading Termcap and Terminfo Entries

Chapter 3 More Termcap and Terminfo Syntax

Chapter 4 Termcap, Terminfo and the Shell

Chapter 5 Writing Termcap and Terminfo Entries

Chapter 6 Converting Between Termcap and Terminfo

Part 2: Capability Reference

Chapter 7 Introduction to the Capabilities

Chapter 8 Screen Dimensions and Cursor Movement

Chapter 9 Editing the Screen

Chapter 10 Initialization and Reset

Chapter 11 Special Effects

Chapter 12 Special Keys

Chapter 13 Padding and XON/XOFF

Chapter 14 Special Terminals

Chapter 15 Equivalent Terminals

Chapter 16 Miscellaneous

Part 3: Appendices

Appendix B Accessing Termcap From a C Program

Appendix C Accessing Terminfo From C Program

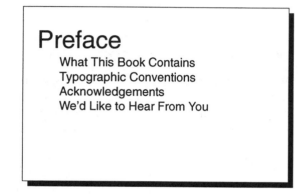

Preface

What This Book Contains
Typographic Conventions
Acknowledgements
We'd Like to Hear From You

A magician never reveals his secret: the unbelievable trick becomes simple and obvious once it is explained. So too with UNIX. Mysterious commands turn out to be rational and orderly once fully revealed. Fortunately, UNIX wizards share their knowledge more readily than their performing brethren.

This book will teach you to understand the language of *termcap* and *terminfo*, the mechanism by which UNIX systems support hundreds of varieties of ASCII terminals without the need for special drivers for each terminal.

After reading this book, you should be able to read and understand a *termcap* or *terminfo* terminal description—and what's more important, you should be able to write a description for a new terminal not supported by your system's current terminal database.

What This Book Contains

The first edition of this book, entitled *Reading and Writing Termcap Entries*, was written in July, 1985 based on a Charles River Data Systems *termcap* system. In the years since then, much has happened! *terminfo* was introduced and *termcap* was greatly expanded. Just over 100 capabilities were supported in our 1985 *termcap* system, versus approximately 300 in System V *terminfo* and BSD 4.3 *termcap*.

With all this growth and change, this book needed a full revision. The main question we faced was whether to document *termcap* and *terminfo* separately in two books or together in one.

We decided on a single book for two reasons. First, most of the capabilities in *termcap* and *terminfo* are identical except in name. Second, some programmers and system administrators must support both systems and may need to convert between *termcap* and *terminfo*.

The price of covering two, albeit closely related, systems under one cover is that some information applies to only one of the systems, and users who only care about one need to weed it out from the description of the other. To minimize this price, information that applies to both systems is described in generic terms, such as "the terminal database" or a "terminal description," while information specific to one of the systems refers to that system by name. Furthermore, we have clearly labeled any section that applies to only one of the systems.

The growth and changes in *termcap* have resulted in various *termcap* systems in different stages of evolution. This book uses *termcap* BSD 4.3 as the standard. In addition, to allow for some future additions to *termcap*, it lists the *termcap* names analogous to the *terminfo* capabilities that are not implemented in BSD 4.3. (These names are used by the System V programs for converting *terminfo* to *termcap*.) We can also expect *terminfo* to have capabilities added in the future. However, the core set of capabilities will be constant, with the additions providing special capabilities for advanced terminal features or capabilities to describe other sorts of output devices.

Some *termcap* users will find that their system only uses a subset of the *termcap* BSD 4.3 capabilities. Those users will need to refer to their system's documentation to see which capabilities apply and which do not.

We believe this book has several advantages over the standard *termcap* and *terminfo* documentation.

- It explains the systems from scratch, assuming you know nothing about them.

- It uses more examples and tables than the standard documentation.

- We have put considerable thought into laying out this book in a clear and logical way. This includes indexing and tabulating. Despite being more voluminous than the standard documentation, this book allows you to find capability information more quickly.

- Many capability descriptions in the system source documentation are brief and cryptic. By combining various sources and people's personal experience, we have been able to fill in most of these holes in the capability descriptions.

- Documenting *termcap* and *terminfo* together provides a tremendous advantage to users converting from one to another or users accustomed to one who have to adjust the other.

- We have put special emphasis on the problems of the terminal owner or system administrator who needs to write or modify a *termcap* or *terminfo* entry for a new terminal.

This book is split into three parts:

- Part 1 (Chapters 1 through 6) is a tutorial on *termcap* and *terminfo*: it describes the development of the two systems and how to read, write, and use the two systems. It also describes the utilities for converting between the two systems.

- Part 2 is the reference section of this book. Chapters 7 through 16 describe the capabilities supported by *termcap* and *terminfo*, grouped into related topics.

- Part 3 contains the four appendices. The appendices include a list of capabilities used by *vi*, methods of accessing *termcap* and *terminfo* from C programs, and a full cross reference of all the capabilities.

At the front of each part is a divider page summarizing the contents of each chapter in that part. There is an index at the end of the book.

Typographic Conventions

The following conventions are used in this book:

italic is used for the names of programs and files where they appear in text.

bold is used in text to highlight the names of *termcap* capabilities.

bold italic is used in text to highlight the names of *terminfo* capabilities.

`courier` is used in examples to show the content of files or the output from system commands.

`courier bold` is used in examples to show commands or text that would be typed in literally by the user.

`courier italic` is used in examples to show variables for which a context-specific substitution should be made. (The variable *`filename`*, for example, would be replaced by some actual filename.) Courier italic is sometimes also used, in parentheses, to highlight comments or an example.

% is the C Shell prompt.

$ is the Bourne Shell prompt.

[ ] surround optional values in a description of program syntax. (The brackets themselves should never be typed.)

You should pay special attention to the distinction between **bold** and ***bold italic***. In many places, the typography will be the only indication of whether a capability is *termcap* or *terminfo*. For example, in the passage:

co#80   says that the terminal has 80 columns
cols#80

co#80 refers to the *termcap* capability definition, while *cols#80* refers
to the *terminfo* equivalent.

A possible point of confusion: in this book, we use the term "capability" to refer both to actual terminal characteristics—for instance, the
number of lines on the screen—and to the *termcap* and *terminfo* syntax
for describing that characteristic. In the latter sense, a capability is the
smallest unit of a *termcap* or *terminfo* description. It should be obvious
from the context when we are referring to an actual terminal characteristic and when to the conventional *termcap* or *terminfo* name for that
characteristic.

Acknowledgements

The original version of this book, *Reading and Writing Termcap
Entries*, was written by John Strang. John also prepared the first draft
of this revised edition. Additional material was supplied by Tim
O'Reilly, and the whole was further rewritten and reorganized by Tim
and Linda Mui. Paul Kleppner wrote the appendices on *termcap* and
terminfo from within a C program.

Sue Willing, Kate Gibson, Daniel Gilly and Ruth Terry provided pro-
duction assistance. Linda Mui extended the standard Nutshell Handbook *troff* macros to reflect the format designed by Sue for the Capability Reference. Donna Woonteiler and Kate Gibson entered the index.

Special thanks to Donna Carroll at Prime Computer for allowing John
and Linda to experiment with their System V Release 3 *terminfo* system; to Paul Kleppner for shedding light on some of the more technical
details; and to Tony Hansen of AT&T for giving us some pointers on
terminal initialization with *tput*. Tony also provided an extensive
technical review, incorporated in this edition.

Some examples and pointers have been taken from the AT&T documentation set and from the GNU Termcap documentation.

We'd Like to Hear From You

We have tested and verified all of the information in this book to the best of our ability, but you may find that features have changed (or even that we have made mistakes!). Please let us know about any errors you find, as well as your suggestions for future editions, by writing:

```
O'Reilly & Associates, Inc.
101 Morris Street
Sebastopol, CA 95472
1-800-998-9938 (in the US or Canada)
1-707-829-0515 (international/local)
1-707-829-0104 (FAX)
```

You can also send us messages electronically. To be put on the mailing list or request a catalog, send email to:

info@oreilly.com   (via the Internet)

To ask technical questions or comment on the book, send email to:

bookquestions@oreilly.com   (via the Internet)

Part 1: Tutorial

This part of the book is a tutorial on *termcap* and *terminfo*. It introduces *termcap* and *terminfo* to the reader and explains how to interpret, write and use terminal entries.

Part 1 consists of six chapters.

Chapter 1, *Introduction*, explains the need for *termcap* and *terminfo* and provides a brief history of their development and an overview of how they are used.

Chapter 2, *Reading Termcap and Terminfo Entries*, provides an introduction to the basic syntax of a terminal entry. The purpose of this chapter is to familiarize you with the "look and feel" of a notably arcane interface. Sample *termcap* and *terminfo* entries are explained so that you can become proficient in reading them.

Chapter 3, *More Termcap and Terminfo Syntax*, describes some of the less intuitive aspects of *termcap* and *terminfo* syntax. Covered in this chapter are encoding arguments and padding.

Chapter 4, *Termcap, Terminfo and the Shell*, describes how the TERM, TERMCAP and TERMINFO environment variables are used to let programs know on what terminal type a user is logged in. Special emphasis is given to the mechanisms available at login. There is also some discussion of the *tput* program, which can be extremely useful in shell scripts to access *terminfo* values.

Chapter 5, *Writing Termcap and Terminfo Entries*, gives advice on how to go about writing a new terminal entry. It includes suggestions for finding existing entries as well as procedures for writing and debugging new entries. It also describes the operation of *tic*, the *terminfo* compiler.

Chapter 6, *Converting Between Termcap and Terminfo*, describes the operation of the *captoinfo* and *infocmp* programs, which can be used for converting between *termcap* and *terminfo*. It also describes some of the comparison functions of *infocmp*.

Introduction

Reading Termcap and Terminfo Entries

More Termcap and Terminfo Syntax

Termcap, Terminfo and the Shell

Writing Termcap and Terminfo Entries

Converting Between Termcap and Terminfo

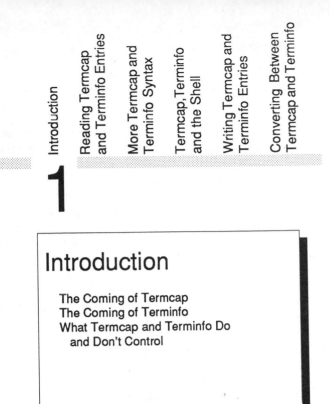

1

Introduction

The Coming of Termcap
The Coming of Terminfo
What Termcap and Terminfo Do
and Don't Control

The Coming of Termcap

Terminals differ. Manufacturers produce a variety of terminals, each one including a particular set of features for a certain price. There are new terminals and old, smart terminals and dumb ones, terminals with big screens and terminals with small screens, printing terminals and video displays, and terminals with all sorts of special features.

Differences between terminals do not matter much to programs like *cat* or *who* that use the terminal screen as a sort of typewriter with an endless scroll of paper. These programs produce sequential output and do not make use of the terminal's special features; they do not need a *termcap* or *terminfo* system. Only programs such as screen editors, which make use of screen-handling features, need to know about differences between terminals.

In the late 1970s, Bill Joy created the *vi* text editor at U.C. Berkeley. Like all screen-oriented editors, *vi* uses the terminal screen non-sequentially. A program performing non-sequential output does not just print character after character, but must manipulate the text that was sent before, scroll the page, move the cursor, delete lines, insert characters, and more. While it would be possible to keep redrawing the screen in its entirety, many features are provided in hardware or firmware by the terminal itself, and save too much time and trouble to be ignored.

The first version of *vi* was written specifically for Lear Siegler ADM3a terminals. *vi* was such an improvement over line-oriented editors that there was great demand to port *vi* to other brands of terminals. The problem was that each terminal had different features and used different control codes to manipulate the features that they did have in common.

Rather than write separate terminal drivers for each terminal type, Bill Joy did the intelligent thing. He wrote a version of *vi* with generic commands to manipulate the screen instead of hard-coding the control codes and dimensions for a particular terminal.

The generic terminal-handling mechanism Joy came up with had two parts: a database describing the capabilities of each of the terminals to be supported, and a subroutine library that allows programs to query that database and to make use of the capability values it contains. Both the library and the database were given the name *termcap*, which is short for *term*inal *cap*abilities.

At this point, users take for granted the fact that you can use just about any terminal with a UNIX system and use screen-oriented programs like *vi* without any problem. But it is really quite remarkable!

If a program is designed to use *termcap* or *terminfo*, it queries an environment variable called TERM to determine the terminal type, then looks up the entry for that terminal in the terminal database, and reads the definition of any capabilities it plans to use into external variables. Programs that use *termcap* or *terminfo* range from screen editors like *vi* and *emacs*, which use the complete terminal description, to a program like *clear*, which needs to know only one capability (the escape sequence to clear the screen). Other programs include *more*, *rogue*, *tset*, *ul* and *nroff*.

The Historical Development of Termcap

Since Joy's initial implementation, *termcap* has grown in three dimensions:

- *termcap* is now used by many more UNIX programs.

- More and more terminals have been described in the *termcap* format—there are now hundreds of terminals in the system *termcap* database, which is kept in the file */etc/termcap*.

- *termcap* has expanded in terms of the number of capability names that can be used to describe terminals.

In order to understand this last point you need to realize that there is no canonical list of terminal capabilities. You can instead think of the capabilities as a language with which system administrators (or whoever else might write a terminal description) can communicate with programmers about how a terminal works. It is also the language that programs use to talk back to the terminal. The routines in the *termcap* library are quite simple: given a terminal type, they allow the program to query whether a given capability is present or absent and what its value is. As new terminals are manufactured, with new capabilities, all that is necessary is for some convention to be established about how to describe that capability.

Non-standard capabilities can also be "invented" by programmers with special needs. For example, the availability of multi-user DOS applications has led to the development of terminals called PC-scancode terminals, that can act like a PC console as well as an ASCII terminal. (PC keyboards do not generate ASCII characters but, rather, separate codes (called scancodes) for the press and release of each key. In addition, the PC screen has 25 lines rather than the usual 24 and can display the special graphic characters of the PC's extended character set.) Programs like Interactive's VP/ix and Locus's Merge 386, which allow DOS to run under UNIX, require the definition of a capability for

5

dynamically switching between ASCII terminal mode and PC-scancode mode, to be used when a DOS program is invoked from UNIX.

A necessary concomitant of this point is that in order for programs to make proper use of a terminal's capabilities, the *termcap* description of those capabilities must be complete and correct. But because *termcap* has grown haphazardly over the years as different members of the UNIX community wrote terminal descriptions, it is not always possible to count on the fact that terminal descriptions will be complete or correct.

That is where this book comes in. It provides the information you need to write entries for new terminals or to complete or correct existing entries.

Termcap and Curses

In contrast to the *termcap* database, which has evolved over the years, the *termcap* library has remained constant.* However, a higher-level subroutine library called *curses* (for "cursor manipulation") was developed to make it easier for programmers to write terminal-independent programs. Programs written with curses use different routines but the same terminal database.

The original version of *curses* was written by Ken Arnold, and is still shipped with BSD systems. The *curses* library was rewritten and expanded by Mark Horton for System V.

Curses is beyond the scope of this book. It is described in another Nutshell Handbook, *Programming with Curses*.

---

* The GNU distribution has developed its own *termcap* library for use by programmers. GNU *termcap* was originally bundled with GNU *emacs*, but is now available separately via anonymous *ftp*. You can get GNU *termcap* from *prep.ai.mit.edu* (18.71.0.38) in the file */pub/gnu/termcap-1.0.tar.Z*.

The Coming of Terminfo

The *terminfo* database is the UNIX System V equivalent to *termcap*, created by Mark Horton. The most important difference between the two systems is that *terminfo* is a compiled database, while *termcap* is a human-readable text database. The *terminfo* approach improves efficiency, but at the price of accessibility. *terminfo* has a greater program support superstructure than *termcap*, but it is not as easy to examine or experiment with.

While the *termcap* database is contained in a single large ASCII file, *terminfo* consists of a directory hierarchy of individual compiled terminal descriptions. In order to view or modify an entry, you must decompile it with a program called *infocmp*; to add an entry, you must write and compile it with *tic*, the *terminfo* compiler, before you can use it. This makes it more difficult to incrementally test a new entry.

On the other hand, *terminfo* had the advantage of being developed with the working model of *termcap* in place. The developers of *terminfo* were able to take a critical look at the capabilities defined for *termcap* and decide which were useful and which were superfluous. They were also able to spot terminal features that were not implemented in *termcap* and to create capability names for them. Thus, *terminfo* does not recognize a few capabilities used by *termcap* (except during *termcap* emulation) but has added support for many new ones.

termcap has also changed its set of capabilities over time, adding names for many of the same new capabilities and defining the capabilities not used by *terminfo* as "obsolete," encouraging programmers to avoid them.

While the capabilities described in both databases are equivalent for the most part, only a few of the capability names are the same. *termcap* allows only two-character capability names, while *terminfo* uses up to five characters. Furthermore, the syntax for encoding some of the more complex capabilities is different.

As of the date of this edition, pure UNIX System V based systems use *terminfo*. Systems based on the Berkeley Software Distribution (BSD 4.x) still use *termcap*. Some systems that incorporate features from both BSD and System V support both *termcap* and *terminfo*.

On these systems, it may be left up to the individual program to decide whether to use *termcap* or *terminfo*. For example, on our Convergent Technologies Miniframe, which uses a version of System V Release 2, *vi* will use either *termcap* or *terminfo* depending on which environment variables are set. However, both the BSD screen pager, *more*, and its System V equivalent, *pg* are provided, and of these, *more* requires a *termcap* entry and *pg* requires a *terminfo* entry. Neither will work if only the other type of entry exists for a terminal.

It is possible to take a program written using *termcap* and relink it with the *terminfo curses* library. This way, even *termcap* programs can in reality be using the *terminfo* database.

What Termcap and Terminfo Do and Don't Control

One important point to realize about *termcap* and *terminfo* is that many programs do not use them at all, and that there are several other mechanisms that may also affect terminal operation.

The operation of the serial interface is controlled by several system files (*/etc/ttys* and */etc/gettytab* on BSD and other non-AT&T systems, and */etc/inittab* and */etc/gettydefs* in System V). Users can affect serial line parameters with the *stty* command. In addition to normal communications parameters such as baud rate, start and stop bits, parity, and so on, these parameters include such things as the translation of the carriage returns generated by most terminals into the linefeeds expected by most UNIX programs, division of input into lines, and definition of special control characters for erasing a character that has been typed, killing a line of typed input, and interrupting a running process.

One other area that *termcap* and *terminfo* do not control is terminal tab setting. This is done by the *tabs*(1) command. For more information, see the man pages on *stty*(1) and *termio*(7) (Sys V).

termcap and *terminfo*, by contrast, tend to control visual attributes of the terminal. The terminal capabilities defined for a terminal tell a screen-oriented program how big the screen is (for screen-by-screen paging and cursor-movement), how to move to any point on the screen, how to refresh the screen, how to enter and exit any special display modes (such as inverse video, blinking, or underlining), and so on.

But there is some overlap. For example, a terminal can be unusable because a program has left either the serial line modes or the terminal itself in an unexpected state. For this reason, terminal initialization, as performed by the *tset* and *tput* programs discussed in Chapter 4, initializes both the terminal and the serial line interface.

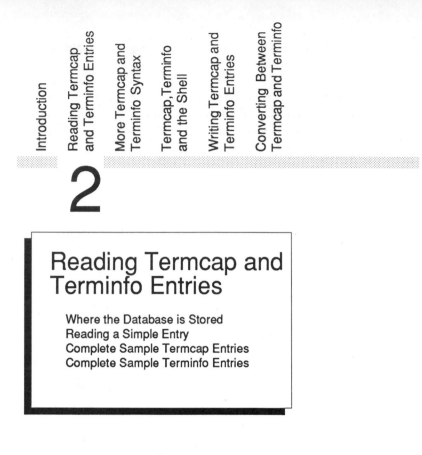

Introduction

Reading Termcap
and Terminfo Entries

More Termcap and
Terminfo Syntax

Termcap, Terminfo
and the Shell

Writing Termcap and
Terminfo Entries

Converting Between
Termcap and Terminfo

2

Reading Termcap and Terminfo Entries

Where the Database is Stored
Reading a Simple Entry
Complete Sample Termcap Entries
Complete Sample Terminfo Entries

In Chapter 1, we described *termcap* and *terminfo* as the language system administrators use to tell programmers about their terminals. This chapter will introduce you to the grammar of this rather terse language. It will explain how the database entries are organized, what sort of capabilities exist, and the format for these capabilities. When you have finished this chapter, you will be able to examine a *termcap* or *terminfo* file and know what to look for in an entry.

This chapter does not teach you what all of the words (capabilities) in the language mean. The description of the capabilities themselves— the vocabulary of the language—is detailed in Part 2 of this book, *Capability Reference*. The purpose of this chapter is to familiarize you with the basic format of *termcap* and *terminfo* entries—to get you to the point where they no longer look like gibberish. Other technical points are covered in Chapter 3, *More Termcap and Terminfo Syntax*.

Where the Database is Stored

The *termcap* terminal database is stored in the single file */etc/termcap*. It is an ASCII file: all the information it contains is readable, if not immediately comprehensible. Each entry consists of a list of names for the terminal, followed by a list of the terminal's capabilities.

The compiled *terminfo* database is stored in a directory hierarchy under */usr/lib/terminfo*. Each terminal entry is compiled (by a program called *tic*) and stored in a separate file. All terminals whose names begin with the letter *a* are stored in the directory */usr/lib/terminfo/a*, and so on through the alphabet.* Entries can be decompiled or displayed with a program called *infocmp*.

A program that wants to make use of the terminal capability database selects an entry according to the value of the TERM environment variable. This variable is typically set when a user logs in. A second variable, either TERMCAP or TERMINFO, may also be set, if it is desirable to point to a terminal description that is not in the standard location.

What Terminal Type are You Using?

To find out what terminal type the system thinks you are currently using, type:

```
% printenv $TERM
```

on a BSD system, or type:

```
$ env | grep $TERM
```

on a System V system.

---

*The source is sometimes provided by some systems in */usr/lib/terminfo.ti*.

Setting the TERM Variable

The TERM variable should be set to the name of a terminal for which a *termcap* or *terminfo* description exists. This is typically done when the user logs in but can be done from the command line as follows:

```
$ TERM=wy50; export TERM      (Bourne shell)
```

or:

```
% setenv TERM wy50            (C shell)
```

(Chapter 4 talks at length about methods for setting TERM during the login process.)

The terminal names to which TERM can legitimately be set can be determined by searching through */etc/termcap* or by listing the names of files in the */usr/lib/terminfo* directory hierarchy.

In *termcap*, the first line of each entry shows several different names, or aliases, for the terminal. At least one of the names will usually reflect the manufacturer's shorthand name for the terminal, but a long name is usually included as well, so you can simply search for the manufacturer's name to get started. For example, if you were using a Wyse Technologies Wyse-50, you could check to make sure that a terminal description for that terminal existed in the *termcap* database by typing:

```
% grep Wyse /etc/termcap
n9|wy50|Wyse Technology WY-50:\
```

One or more lines like the one shown in the example above should be printed (if any matching entries are found). Each line will show several names for the terminal, separated by vertical bars (|). The second name, wy50, is the one most commonly used as the value of TERM. We'll talk more about the other names later in this chapter.

On a system supporting *terminfo*, you would look for the entry with the ls command:

```
$ ls /usr/lib/terminfo/w
wy-50
wy100
wy50
wyse-50
wyse50
```

You should use the name of the appropriate file for the value of TERM. Note that in the case of *terminfo*, there will be a separate filename for each terminal alias. You can use any of these equivalent names.

If it is not obvious from the name of the file which entry to use, you can use the following command to print out the long name of the terminal:

```
$ tput -Tname longname
```

For example:

```
$ tput -Twy50 longname
```

tput will be described further in Chapter 4.

You should be aware that for a terminal with configurable options (such as a terminal with an 80 or 132 column mode), there may be several *termcap* or *terminfo* entries. Until you know enough about the terminal database to compare the entries and find out how they differ, you will simply need to take your chances. Experiment with each of the entries and see which works best.

Displaying a Terminfo Entry

On most systems, *terminfo* is shipped only in compiled form. In order to display the contents of a *terminfo* entry, you can use a program called *infocmp*, available on System V Releases 3 and 4. *infocmp*, however, is not available on all previous System V releases or System-V derived systems. This can put you in quite a pickle if you want to work with *terminfo*.

Fortunately, source for *infocmp* is available for a minimal cost from the AT&T Toolchest. (Call 1-908-522-6900 and login as "guest" (there is no password) to browse through the Toolchest.) While you're there, the source for the *captoinfo* program described in Chapter 6 is also available from the Toolchest. Both *infocmp* and *captoinfo* were written by Tony Hansen of AT&T.

(As an alternative, public domain versions of *infocmp* and *captoinfo* are available on many FTP sites, under the names *untic* and *tctoti*.)

Assuming you have *infocmp*, here is how you would display the uncompiled contents of an entry:

    $ infocmp termname

(If *termname* is not specified, the current value of TERM will be used.)

The *terminfo* description will automatically be retrieved from the appropriate place in the */usr/lib/terminfo*. When using *infocmp*, you should be aware that capabilities which were commented out were stripped from the entry when it was originally compiled and cannot be recovered when it is decompiled.

The *infocmp* program has many functions available. Although its default is to translate the entry into its uncompiled format (the *-I* option), it was designed primarily to compare two *terminfo* entries. It can also be used for providing long names for capabilities and, of particular interest to this book, for converting a *terminfo* entry into *termcap* syntax. Chapter 6 has more information on the many uses of *infocmp*.

Reading a Simple Entry

Let us begin our study of the language of *termcap* and *terminfo* by reading a simplified entry for the Wyse Technology Wyse-50 terminal. (The full entry for the Wyse-50 is shown at the end of this chapter.) The capabilities described here are only a subset sufficient to introduce the basic syntax of the language.

Here is the *termcap* entry:

```
# incomplete termcap entry for the Wyse WY-50
n9|wy50|WY50| Wyse Technology WY-50:\
     :bs:am:co#80:li#24:\
     :up=^K:cl=^Z:ho=^^:nd=^L:cm=\E=% %+ :
```

And here is the corresponding *terminfo* sourcefile:

```
# incomplete terminfo entry for Wyse WY-50
wy50|WY50|Wyse Technology WY-50,
     am, cols#80, lines#24, cuu1=^K, clear=^Z,
     home=^^, cuf1=^L, cup=\E=%p1%'\s'%+%c%p2%'\s'%+%c,
```

The backslash character is used to suppress the newline in *termcap*. *termcap* entries must be defined on a single logical line, with colons (:) separating each field. *terminfo* does not require the entry to be on a single line, so backslashes are not necessary. In *terminfo*, commas are used as the field separator.

The language certainly is not verbose! However, if we work through it methodically, it might begin to make sense.

There are three types of lines in a *termcap* or *terminfo* file: comment lines, lines that list alias names for the terminal, and lines that specify terminal capabilities.

- *Comment Lines:*
  The first line in both the *termcap* and *terminfo* entries shown above is a comment line.

      # incomplete termcap entry for the Wyse WY-50
      # incomplete terminfo entry for the Wyse WY-50

  All comment lines begin with a sharp sign. Embedded comments are not allowed: a line is either a comment or part of an entry. In *termcap* and *terminfo*, the convention is that comments precede the terminal they describe.

- *Name Lines:*
  The second line is a list of alias names for the terminal, separated by the vertical bar character.

      n9|wy50|WY50| Wyse Technology WY-50:\   (termcap)

      wy50|WY50|Wyse Technology WY-50,   (terminfo)

  Multiple aliases are provided as a convenience to the user. The environment variable TERM can be set to any one of the aliases. By convention, the last alias is the full name of the terminal. There are other conventions for naming terminals, discussed more fully in Chapter 5.

  The alias list is the first field of the terminal description, with a colon (*termcap*) or comma (*terminfo*) marking the end of the alias list and the start of the capabilities list. You could begin listing the capabilities immediately after this field, but it makes reading much easier if all the aliases are on one line and the capabilities start on the next.

When a *terminfo* source file is compiled with *tic*, the compiled data is placed in a file corresponding to the first alias (in this case, */usr/lib/terminfo/w/wy50*), and a link is created for all other aliases but the last. In this example, TERM could be set to either *wy50* or *WY50* to access the compiled terminal description.

See Chapter 5 for more information on naming conventions in *termcap* and *terminfo*.

* *Capability Lines:*
  The remaining lines are the list of the actual terminal capabilities. These lines are indented (using a tab or blank spaces) to distinguish them from the line of terminal aliases. Note that the indentation of continued capability lines is not just cosmetic but is a required part of the syntax.

In *termcap*, capabilities are identified by a two-character name; in *terminfo*, the capability names may have anywhere between two and five characters. The capability name is the first thing in each capability field and describes a feature of the terminal.

There are three types of capability:

* **Boolean capabilities** consist of a capability name with no arguments. For example, **am** (both *termcap* and *terminfo*) specifies that the terminal performs automatic right margins, wrapping the cursor to the start of the next line when the cursor reaches the last position on the current line. If **am** is not specified, programs will assume that your terminal does not have this feature.

  am is an example of a Boolean feature which is advantageous, but Booleans are also used to specify negative features of your terminal—for example, if your terminal does not perform newlines in the expected way, you might have what is called the "newline glitch", and you may need to specify **xn** (*termcap*) or *xenl* (*terminfo*) to tell programs to adjust for your peculiarity.

* **Numeric capabilities** consist of a capability name, a sharp sign, and a number. For example, **co#80** (*termcap*) and *cols#80* (*terminfo*) says that the terminal has 80 columns. All numeric values are non-negative.

- **String capabilities** tell how to issue a command to the terminal. The format of a string capability is the capability name followed by an equals sign followed by the command sequence. For example, **up=^K** (*termcap*) or **cuu1=^K** (*terminfo*) specifies that the sequence CTRL-K will move the cursor up one line.

Now the Wyse-50 example should make more sense. First *termcap*:

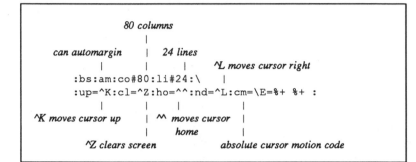

Now *terminfo*:

The examples demonstrate all three kinds of capabilities: Boolean, numeric, and string.

The first two capabilities in the *termcap* entry, and the first capability in the *terminfo* entry, are Boolean.

bs   is the *termcap* backspace capability, which means that the terminal will backspace when sent the CTRL-H (^H) character. There is no *terminfo* capability directly equivalent to

bs, so it is considered obsolete by *terminfo* and by BSD 4.3 *termcap*. In place of the **bs** capability, *terminfo* would explicitly define CTRL-H as the string to send the cursor left (*cul1=^H*).

am   is the automargin capability, also known as wraparound. It
am   means that when a line reaches the right edge of the screen, the terminal automatically continues on the next line.

The next two capabilities are numeric.

co#80   says that the terminal has 80 columns.
cols#80

li#24   says that the terminal has 24 lines.
lines#24

You will find that 80 characters and 24 lines is the most common screen size but that there are exceptions. Eighty characters was originally chosen because it is the width of a punch card, and 24 lines was chosen to take advantage of cheap television screen technology.

The remainder of the fields in the Wyse-50 entry contain string capabilities. The first four of these are fairly simple:

up=^K   is the up capability; it says that to move the cursor up one
cuu1=^K   line, send the ^K character to the terminal.

cl=^Z   is the clear capability; it says that to clear the screen, send
clear=^Z   the ^Z character to the terminal.

ho=^^   is the home capability; it says that to move the cursor
*home=^^*   Home (upper left corner), send the ^^ character (CTRL-^) to the terminal.

nd=^L   is the non-destructive space capability; it says that to move
cuf1=^L   the cursor one space to the right without changing the text, send the ^L character to the terminal.

Special Character Codes

No doubt the symbols ^K, ^Z, ^^, and ^L shown above are familiar to you. A caret (^) followed by a letter is a convention for representing an unprintable control character generated by holding down the Control (CTRL) key on the keyboard while typing another. Note that control characters are entered into a terminal description as two characters by typing the caret character (^) followed by a letter, rather than by insert-ing the actual control character.

Both *termcap* and *terminfo* use other codes to write other unprintable characters, as well as characters that have special meaning in *termcap* or *terminfo* syntax. The other codes, most of which should be familiar to C programmers, are listed in the table below.

Code	Description	Comment
\E	escape	*termcap and terminfo*
\e	escape	*terminfo only*
^*x*	control-*x*	*where x is any letter*
\n	newline	
\r	return	
\t	tab	
\b	backspace	
\f	formfeed	
\s	space	*terminfo only*
\l	linefeed	*terminfo only*
xxx	octal value of *xxx*	*must be three characters*
\041	exclamation point '!'	*C-shell history uses '!'*
\072	the character ':'	*termcap uses ordinary : as separator*
\200	null	*\000 for null does not work*
\0	null	*terminfo only*
\^	caret	*terminfo only*
\\	backslash	*terminfo only*
\,	comma	*terminfo only*
\:	colon	*terminfo only*

Encoding Arguments

The last capability in the Wyse-50 example is the most complicated. cm= (*termcap*) and cup= (*terminfo*) specify the cursor motion capabil-ity, which describes how to move the cursor directly to a specific loca-tion. Since the desired location is specified by the program at run time, the capability must provide some mechanism for encoding arguments. The program uses this description to figure out what string it needs to send to move the cursor to the desired location.

Argument encoding is more fully explained in Chapter 3, *More Termcap and Terminfo Syntax*. For the purposes of this chapter, you should just know that the percent sign (%) is used for encoding, and when it appears in a terminal entry, the capability is using run time parameters.

Complete Sample Termcap Entries

In this section, sample *termcap* entries are provided for several terminals. The equivalent *terminfo* entries are shown in the next section of this chapter.

The capabilities for these terminals are individually described following the entry. To make it easier to correlate the entry with the commentary that follows, each of the capability lines is numbered. **These line numbers are <u>not</u> a part of the entry.**

Wyse 50

The first example shows a complete entry for the Wyse Technology Wyse-50 terminal.

```
   n9|wy50|Wyse Technology WY-50:\
1     :li#24:co#80:am:bs:bw:ul:\
2     :cm=\E=%+ %+ :\
3     :nd=^L:up=^K:do=^J:ho=^^:bt=\EI:\
4     :cl=^Z:ce=\ET:cd=\EY:\
5     :al=\EE:dl=\ER:ic=\EQ:dc=\EW:\
6     :so=\EG4:se=\EG0:sg#1:\
7     :ue=\EG0:us=\EG8:ug#1\
8     :kl=^H:kr=^L:ku=^K:kd=^J:kh=^^:\
9     :k1=^A@^M:k2=^AA^M:k3=^AB^M:k4=^AC^M:k5=^AD^M:\
10    :k6=^AE^M:k7=^AF^M:k8=^AG^M:k9=^AH^M:k0=^AI^M:
```

The first line in the entry is the list of aliases. The rest of the lines contain a list of terminal capabilities.

Line 1: Basic Capabilities

li#24	Screen has 24 lines.
co#80	Screen has 80 columns.
am	Terminal has automargin (wraparound).
bs	CTRL-H is backspace.
bw	Can backspace to previous line.
ul	Can underline but not overstrike.

Line 2: Absolute Cursor Motion

cm=\E=%+ %+   Describes sequence for cursor motion.

Line 3: Relative Cursor Motion

nd=^L	CTRL-L moves cursor to the right.
up=^K	CTRL-K moves cursor up.
do=^J	CTRL-J moves cursor down.
ho=^^	CTRL-^ moves cursor home.
bt=\EI	ESC-I moves to the previous tab stop.

Line 4: Clearing

cl=^Z	CTRL-Z clears screen from cursor to upper left.
ce=\ET	ESC-T clears to the end of the line.
cd=\EY	ESC-Y clears the display after cursor.

Line 5: Adding and Deleting

al=\EE	ESC-E adds a line above cursor.
dl=\ER	ESC-R deletes the current line.
ic=\EQ	ESC-Q inserts a single blank space.
dc=\EW	ESC-W deletes character at cursor.

Line 6: Standout Mode

so=\EG4	ESC-G4 begins standout mode.
se=\EG0	ESC-G0 ends standout mode.
sg#1	When changing to standout mode, one additional space is output.

Line 7: Underline Mode

ue=\EG0	ESC-G0 ends underline mode.
us=\EG8	ESC-G8 begins underline mode.
ug#1	When changing to underline mode, one additional space is output.

Line 8: Arrow Keys

kl=^H	CTRL-H is sent by the left arrow key.
kr=^L	CTRL-L is sent by the right arrow key.
ku=^K	CTRL-K is sent by the up arrow key.
kd=^J	CTRL-J is sent by the down arrow key.
kh=^^	CTRL-^ is sent by the home key.

Lines 9 and 10: Function Key Definitions

The ten function key capabilities (**k1-k0**) send two characters, a CTRL-A and another character (A through I or @), followed by a carriage return (^M). For example, function key 1 sends the sequence ^A@^M, function key 2 sends ^AA^M, and function key 10 sends ^AI^M. Since the Wyse-50 has no function key F0, we are using the **k0=** capability to refer to function key F10.

DEC vt52

As an example of a simpler terminal, the entry for Digital Equipment Corporation's vt52 is show below.

```
  dv|vt52|dec vt52\
1   :cr=^M:do=^J:nl=^J:\
2   :bs:cd=\EJ:ce=\EK:cl=\EH\EJ:cm=\EY%+ %+ :co#80:li#24:nd=\EC:\
3   :ta=^I:pt:sr=\EI:up=\EA:ku=\EA:kd=\EB:kr=\EC:kl=\ED:kb=^H:
```

Line 1:

cr=^M	Carriage return is CTRL-M.
do=^J	CTRL-J moves the cursor down.
nl=^J	CTRL-J is a newline.

Line 2:

bs	CTRL-H backspaces.
cd=\EJ	ESC-J clears display after cursor.
ce=\EK	ESC-K clears to the end of line.
cl=\EH\EJ	ESC-H, ESC-J clears screen from cursor to upper left.
cm=\EY%+ %+	Send sequence ESC-Y followed by the sum of an ASCII space and the desired row and column.
co#80	Screen has 80 columns.
li#24	Screen has 24 lines.
nd=\EC	ESC-C moves cursor to the right.

Line 3:

ta=^I	Tab character is CTRL-I.
pt	CTRL-I moves cursor to next tab position.
sr=\EI	ESC-I scrolls backwards one line.
up=\EA	ESC-A moves cursor up.
ku=\EA	ESC-A is sent by up arrow key.
kd=\EB	ESC-B is sent by down arrow key.
kr=\EC	ESC-C is sent by right arrow key.
kl=\ED	ESC-D is sent by left arrow key.
kb=^H	Backspace key sends CTRL-H.

A Generic Dumb Terminal

Every *termcap* file includes a definition of a generic terminal type, with minimal capabilities, which can be used when the real terminal type is unknown. This description will allow programs other than screen-editors to function. It might look something like this:

```
su|unknown|switch|dialup|arpanet|network|net:\
    :am:bl=^G:co#80:cr=^M:do=^J:nl=^J:
```

am	Terminal has automargin (wraparound).
bl=^G	Terminal bell is rung by CTRL-G.
co#80	Screen has 80 columns.
cr=^M	Carriage return is CTRL-M.

do=^J	Down is CTRL-J.
nl=^J	Newline is CTRL-J.

These generic entries are a last resort, and a mechanism exists for determining a preferable terminal if a generic terminal type is specified. A program called *tset* allows generic entries to be mapped to other entries based on criteria such as baud rate, or for a *.profile* or *.login* file to prompt the user. This mechanism is described in Chapter 4.

BSD 4.3 *termcap* also includes a Boolean capability called **gn**, which is short for generic. It tells programs that they are working with a generic entry, so if a program is unable to perform a task, it can ask the user to specify what terminal type they are really using. (In contrast, some terminals are just plain weak, and there is no point in asking the user to specify the terminal type.)

Complete Sample Terminfo Entries

The following section gives annotated *terminfo* entries for several terminals.

Wyse 50

```
   wy50|Wyse Technology WY-50,
1     bw,    am,    ul,
2     cols#80,    lines#24,
3     bel=^G,    cr=\r,    cud1=\n,
4     cub1=\b,    kbs=\b,    kcud1=\n,
5     kcub1=\b,    nel=\r\n,    ind=\n,
6     xmc#1,    cbt=\EI,
7     clear=^Z,    el=\ET,    ed=\EY,
8     cup=\E=%p1%'\s'%+%c%p2%'\s'%+%c,
9     cuf1=\f,    cuu1=^K,    home=^^,
10    dch1=\EW,    dl1=\ER,    smso=\EG4,
11    smul=\EG8,    rmso=\EG0,    rmul=\EG0,
12    ich1=\EQ,    il1=\EE,
13    kf0=^AI\r,    kf1=^A@\r,
14    kf2=^AA\r,    kf3=^AB\r,    kf4=^AC\r,
15    kf5=^AD\r,    kf6=^AE\r,    kf7=^AF\r,
16    kf8=^AG\r,    kf9=^AH\r,
17    kcub1=\b,    kcuf1=\f,    kcuu1=^K,
```

Line 1: Boolean Capabilities

bw	Terminal has backwards wrap.
am	Terminal does automatic margin.
ul	Terminal can underline.

Line 2: Numeric Capabilities

cols#80	Terminal has 80 columns.
lines#24	Terminal has 24 lines.

Line 3: String Capabilities

bel=^G	CTRL-G gives the audio bell.
cr=\r	Return is the carriage return.
cud1=\n	Newline brings cursor down one row.

Line 4:

cub1=\b	Backspace brings cursor back one column.
kbs=\b	Backspace key sends backspace.
kcud1=\n	Down arrow key sends newline.

Line 5:

kcub1=\b	Left arrow key sends backspace.
nel=\r\n	Newline is carriage return and newline.
ind=\n	Scroll forward with newline.

Line 6:

xmc#1	Magic cookie glitch is one character.
cbt=\EI	ESC-I gives a back tab.

Line 7:

clear=^Z	Clear screen with CTRL-Z.
el=\ET	Clear to end of line with ESC-T.
ed=\EY	Clear to end of display with ESC-Y.

Line 8:

cup=\E=%p1%' '%+%c%p2%' '%+%c

    Send ESC-= followed by the ASCII sums of a space and the desired row and column.

*home=^^*   CTRL-^ sends cursor to home (upper left).

Line 9:
cuf1=\f   Formfeed brings cursor forward one column.
cuu1=^K   CTRL-K brings cursor up one row.

Line 10:
dch1=\EW   Delete one character with ESC-W.
dl1=\ER   Delete one line with ESC-R.
smso=\EG4   Enter standout mode with ESC-G4.

Line 11:
smul=\EG8   Enter underline mode with ESC-G8.
rmso=\EG0   Exit standout mode with ESC-G0.
rmul=\EG0   Exit underline mode with ESC-G0.

Line 12:
ich1=\EQ   Insert one character with ESC-Q.
il1=\EE   Insert one line with ESC-E.

Line 13:
kf0=^AI\r   Tenth function key sends CTRL-A I return.
kf10=^A@\r   First function key sends CTRL-A @ return.

Line 14:
kf2=^AA\r   Second function key sends CTRL-A A return.
kf3=^AB\r   Third function key sends CTRL-A B return.
kf4=^AC\r   Fourth function key sends CTRL-A C return.

Line 15:
kf5=^AD\r   Fifth function key sends CTRL-A D return.
kf6=^AE\r   Sixth function key sends CTRL-A E return.
kf7=^AF\r   Seventh function key sends CTRL-A F return.

Line 16:
kf8=^AG\r   Eighth function key sends CTRL-A G return.
kf9=^AH\r   Ninth function key sends CTRL-A H return.

Line 17:
kcub1=\b   Left arrow key sends backspace.
kcuf1=\f   Up arrow key sends formfeed.

DEC vt52

```
vt52|dec vt52\   ,
1     cols#80,    lines#24,
2     bel=^G,     cr=\r,      clear=\EH\EJ,
3     el=\EK,     ed=\EJ,     cup=\EY%p1%' '%+%c%p2%' '%+%c,
4     cud1=\n,    cub1=\b,    cuf1=\EC,
5     cuu1=\EA,   kbs=\b,     kcud1=\EB,
6     kcub1=\ED,  kcuf1=\EC,  kcuu1=\EA,
7     nel=\r\n,   ind=\n,     ri=\EI,
8     ht=\t,
```

Line 1:

cols#80	Terminal has 80 columns.
lines#24	Terminal has 24 lines.

Line 2:

bel=^G	CTRL-G produces audio bell.
cr=\r	Return is carriage return.
clear=\EH\EJ	Clear screen with ESC-H-ESC-J.

Line 3:

el=\EK	Clear to end of line with ESC-K.
ed=\EJ	Clear to end of display with ESC-J.
cup=\EY%p1%'\s'%+%c%p2%'\s'%+%c	
	Send ESC-Y followed by the ASCII sums of a space and the desired row and column.

Line 4:

cud1=\n	Newline brings cursor down one row.
cub1=\b	Backspace brings cursor left one column.
cuf1=\EC	ESC-C brings cursor forward one column.

Line 5:

cuu1=\EA	ESC-A brings cursor up one row.
kbs=\b	Backspace is backspace character.
kcud1=\EB	Down arrow key sends ESC-B.

Line 6:

kcub1=\ED	Left arrow key sends ESC-D.
kcuf1=\EC	Right arrow key sends ESC-C.
kcuu1=\EA	Up arrow key sends ESC-A.

Line 7:

nel=\r\n   Newline is a return and a newline.
ind=\n   Newline scrolls down one line.
ri=\EI   ESC-I scrolls up one line.

Line 8:
ht=\t   Tab is hard tab character.

A Generic Dumb Terminal

Every *terminfo* file includes a definition of a generic terminal type, with minimal capabilities, which can be used when the real terminal type is unknown. On the Prime EXL-316, it looks like this:

```
unknown|switch|intelligent switch|dialup|arpanet|network|net,
1    am, gn,
2    cols#80,
3    bel=^G, cr=\r, cud1=\en, ind=\en,
```

Line 1:
am   Terminal has automargin.
gn   Terminal is generic.

Line 2:
cols#80   Terminal has 80 columns.

Line 3:
bel=^G   CTRL-G rings keyboard bell.
cr=\r   Return performs carriage return.
cud1=\n   Newline brings cursor down one row.
ind=\n   Newline scrolls down one line.

As it turns out, these generic entries are a last resort, and a mechanism exists for determining a preferable terminal if a generic terminal type is specified.

The *gn* capability is short for generic. It tells the programs that they are working with a generic entry, so if a program is unable to perform a task, it can ask the user to specify what terminal type they are really using. (In contrast, some terminals are just plain weak, and there is no point in asking the user to specify the terminal type.) In *terminfo* systems, the *tput* command could be used in a *.profile* to test for the presence of this capability, and prompt the user for a better terminal type. See Chapter 4 for more information on *tput*.

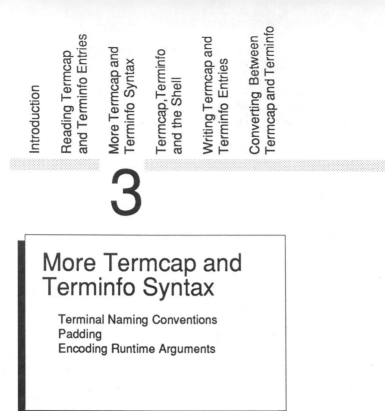

Introduction

Reading Termcap
and Terminfo Entries

More Termcap and
Terminfo Syntax

Termcap, Terminfo
and the Shell

Writing Termcap and
Terminfo Entries

Converting Between
Termcap and Terminfo

3

More Termcap and
Terminfo Syntax

Terminal Naming Conventions
Padding
Encoding Runtime Arguments

This chapter covers the syntax details which we deemed too complex to cover in Chapter 2. Chapter 2 was designed to help novice system administrators get their feet wet with *termcap* and *terminfo*, without scaring them off. This chapter will shed a little more light on some of the topics we skimmed.

The topics we discuss in this chapter are terminal naming conventions, padding, and encoding arguments. Argument encoding can get to be very hairy, especially for *terminfo* entries. Padding is fairly easy to specify but can cause problems when trying to decide when to specify it and how much is needed.

Terminal Naming Conventions

When we first looked at the syntax of entries, the terminal name line was presented as multiple aliases for the terminal. In fact, there is a standard pattern for those aliases, although it is not rigorously enforced. Here is a good example:

```
c2|c108|c108-8p|concept 108 w/8 pages:\     (termcap)

c108|c108-8p|concept 108 w/8 pages,         (terminfo)
```

For *termcap*, the first alias is always two characters, of which the first character identifies the manufacturer and the second (usually an integer) identifies the terminal. The second *termcap* name is the most common canonical name for the terminal model or mode for a terminal model. The last alias is a verbose description of the terminal. Any additional aliases should come between the third and the verbose alias. By convention, aliases should be in lower case, although some manufacturers have been assigned a capital one-letter abbreviation. (IBM's one letter abbreviation is a big I. Could it possibly be anything else?)

The naming convention for *terminfo* is slightly different than that for *termcap*. There is no two-character name equivalent to the first *termcap* name. The first *terminfo* name is the most common abbreviation for the terminal. The last *terminfo* name is the verbose, fully descriptive name of the terminal. All other names for the terminal are put in between.

There are a few additional conventions: All names should be unique, only the last, verbose name should contain spaces, and terminal names should not include a dash "-" except when using terminal flags (more on that in a moment). In *terminfo*, names for entries that are only for use by other entries through the *terminfo* **use=** capability should contain a "+" sign in their name.

Naming Flags

The example shown above also demonstrates another convention for terminal aliases. The third alias has two parts, separated by the dash "-". The first part is the manufacturer's name and the model concatenated together. The second part is a description of the hardware modes or options of the terminal.

Many terminals can be set up to run in different modes with hardware or software options. You can write different terminal entries for the different setup options and issue the software commands to configure the terminal that way in the initialization capabilities. (See the description of the initialization capabilities in Part 2.) The naming convention for terminals with varying setup options uses flags separated by hyphens to identify options that are set. For example, the Digital vt100 set to use wide mode uses the name "vt100-w".

There are some conventions that are followed in using flags for hardware setup modes. The standard suffix flags are:

-am   Terminal is set up to perform automatic margins.

-nam Terminal is set up so that it does not perform automatic margins.

-w   Terminal is set up in wide mode with more than the usual number of columns.

-rv   Terminal is set up in reverse video mode. Normal output is output in reverse video mode, and output specified as reverse video is output in normal mode.

-na   Terminal is set up with "no arrows." In other words, the arrow keypad is put into local mode.

-s   Terminal is set up with "status" line. This is for terminals which can take one or more lines which are normally used as part of the screen proper and use them as status lines. It is **not** for terminals which have permanently dedicated status lines which they can turn off and on.

-*n*   Terminal is set up to operate with *n* lines only. For example, the Ann Arbor Ambassador can be configured to run with between 20 and 60 lines, using smaller characters when using more lines. Users have their own preferences, probably based on the acuity of their eyesight.

-*n*p   Terminal has *n* pages of screen memory set up as a hardware option.

-unk   Terminal has "unknown" modes. The entry is for the general description of a terminal which has several of the other modes described above. Those entries can then use the equivalent terminal capability to read in this generic description and add their own customizations. Those entries would then have their own specific naming flags. See Chapter 15 for more information on assigning equivalent terminals.

When writing entries, you may find it necessary to make up your own flags, depending on your terminals. The flags should not describe the terminal in full—that is the purpose of the entry itself. They are for distinguishing different setup options of a single model.

If more than one flag applies, concatenate them together. The dashes between flags are sometimes, but not always, dropped. Provide alias names with the flags in either order so that the user does not have to remember the order of the flags. An example of a name line that shows an alias with multiple flags is:

```
dt|vt100-w-nam|vt100-nam-w|vt100 132 colw/advanced video:\   (termcap)

vt100-w-nam|vt100-nam-w|vt100 132 colw/advanced video,      (terminfo)
```

Padding

Some terminals need time to digest certain commands: they cannot receive further output from a program until they finish processing the current output. This extra time is called *padding*. Programs pad commands by sending an appropriate number of "no-op" characters (usually the null character). These "no-ops" are ignored, giving the terminal time to complete the command.

For example, say a terminal is running at 9600 baud, has capacity to buffer 20 input characters, and needs 50 milliseconds to perform an absolute cursor movement command. It receives the absolute cursor movement command. For the next 100 milliseconds, it must buffer input in its 10-character buffer. During that time, the computer could send (9600 baud) * (.05 second) / (8 bits/character) = 60 characters. Only the first 20 characters could be handled—the rest would be lost. Therefore, this terminal would need to pad the absolute movement capability for at least 33.3 milliseconds. If the terminal was attached at 19200 baud, the padding requirement would increase to 41.7 milliseconds. One could be conservative and specify the padding requirement as a full 50 milliseconds.*

The amount of time a terminal takes to do a command is terminal-dependent, so there are no general rules defining which capabilities should be padded and by how much. Chapter 5 gives some information on how to determine whether your capability has the right amount of padding specified. Note that adding extra padding will never hurt—it will just slow down the display by the specified amount. Omitting padding that is needed will result in characters being lost when the terminal runs out of buffer space for receiving characters while busy executing a command.

Padding Syntax in Termcap

termcap indicates padding by specifying the delay time in milliseconds after the equal sign and before the command code in a string capability. For example, **ho=10^^** would indicate a delay of 10 milliseconds after the cursor is moved to the "home" position with the ^^ (CTRL-caret) command.

It is also possible to specify proportional padding, which means that the delay should be applied to each line that is affected. This is done by following the padding value with an asterisk. For example, if the clear screen capability were specified as **cl=5.5*^Z** on a 24 line screen, a wait of 5.5 * 24 = 132 milliseconds occurs after a ^Z is sent to allow the screen to clear.

---

*The tputs() function is the C library function actually used by programs to output padding. (tputs() is described in Appendix B.) tputs() sends null characters for the appropriate time interval—the null characters are thrown away by the terminal. tputs() is smart enough to adjust the number of pad characters it sends to the baud rate. Therefore, the padding you specify really does represent a time interval.

One place to the right of the decimal point is allowed for proportional padding. If an integer value is specified, the decimal point can be omitted. In *termcap*, the padding is always output after the string.

Padding Syntax in Terminfo

terminfo indicates padding in a slightly different way. Padding is written as:

```
$<n*>
```

where *n* is the amount of padding and * is an optional flag indicating proportional padding. Proportional padding in *terminfo* works identical to the way it does in *termcap*: it is represented by the asterisk and the delay will be applied to each line. If the clear screen capability in *terminfo* were *clear=^Z* on a 24-line screen, a wait of 5.5 * 24 = 132 milliseconds occurs after ^Z is sent to clear the line.

Thus, an example of padded capabilities might be:

```
clear=^Z$<5.5*>,    home=^^$<10>
```

The $<*pad*> bracket can be put anywhere in the *terminfo* capability. The padding will be transmitted at that point within the string. Since the padding is usually desired after a sequence, the padding is usually placed at the end of the capability.

Sometimes it makes more sense elsewhere. For example, a clear screen capability may be created using two escape sequences: ESC-H to move the home position, which requires a 20-millisecond pad; and ESC-L to clear from there to the end of the screen, which requires a 30-millisecond pad. In *termcap*, the two pads would have to be combined together, as in:

```
cl=50\EH\EL
```

while in *terminfo*, the padding is kept where it belongs, as in:

```
clear=\EH$<20>\EL$<30>
```

and will be subsequently output at the correct time.

XON/XOFF Flow Control

XON/XOFF is a system which controls the flow of data between a sender and a receiver. In XON/XOFF, the terminal sends the XOFF character (usually ^S) when it can not handle any more input, and the XON (usually ^Q) character when it is ready for input again. If the terminal uses XON/XOFF, then programs should use the XON/XOFF protocol instead of sending padding.

In the XON/XOFF system, the terminal runs the system. If the terminal needs a pause, it sends the XOFF character to the computer. The computer stops transmitting data when it detects the XOFF character. When the terminal is ready for more data, it sends the XON character and the computer resumes transmission.

Systems that use the XON/XOFF protocol should still use padding information. Although padding characters are not sent, the padding information can be used to calculate what is the fastest way to accomplish a given function. Programs should be able to figure out which method is faster for accomplishing the same task and then choose the faster capability, as it will go into XOFF mode for the shortest time. For example, in *termcap*, if the parameterized line-adding capability **AL=** needs a 35-millisecond pad no matter how many lines are added, and the non-parameterized version **al=** requires a 10-millisecond pad each time it is used, then a smart program would use **al=** to add three or less lines and **AL=** to add four or more.

Padding information should therefore be included even for terminals which use XON/XOFF, so that they can calculate the time cost of the capabilities.

Mandatory Padding (Terminfo only)

In *terminfo*, the / character can be included in *terminfo* padding specifications to indicate "mandatory padding." Mandatory padding is padding which is sent even when the terminal is in XON/XOFF mode. For example, we could have specified:

```
clear=^Z$<5.5*/>, home=^^$<10/>
```

Mandatory padding is available in *terminfo* only, System V Release 3 and later. (System V Release 2 will treat it as optional.)

The *termcap* (**pc**) and *terminfo* (*pad*) capability specifies the pad character to use instead of the null character. Many terminals use a delete character (octal 177) instead. *terminfo* also supplies *npc* to say that there is no character which can be used as a pad character.

Encoding Run Time Arguments

In Chapter 2, we used an entry for the Wyse Technologies Wyse-50 to demonstrate the format of a *termcap* or *terminfo* entry and to show some different types of capability. The last capability in the Wyse example was the cursor movement capability (*cup=* in *terminfo* and **cm=** in *termcap*), which was not explained in full. We will try to explain it in full here.

cm= (*termcap*) and *cup=* (*terminfo*) are the cursor motion capabilities, which describe how to move the cursor directly to a specific location. Since the desired location is specified by the program at run time, the capability must provide some mechanism for describing arguments. The program uses this description to figure out what string it needs to send to move the cursor to the desired location.

Other capabilities that require run time parameters include parameterized line deletion (delete a run time-specified number of lines), changing the scrolling region (scroll only the part of the screen between the two specified lines), programming function keys (program the specified function key to send a specified string), and setting windows (set a window on the screen between two specified rows and two specified columns).

An important distinction that deserves emphasis is that simple string capabilities tell what string to send, while string capabilities with arguments tell the program how to calculate what string to send.

The cursor movement capabilities for the Wyse-50 appear as follows:

```
:cm=\E=%+ %+ :                        (termcap)
cup=\E=%p1%'\s'%+%c%p2%'\s'%+%c,       (terminfo)
```

The *termcap* and *terminfo* strings are quite different! They contain the same information, but they have different syntaxes for describing run time arguments. The *terminfo* syntax is much more complicated than the *termcap* syntax, so we will examine the *termcap* **cm=** capability first.

Parameters in Termcap

In the example above, let's look at the termcap description for cursor movement. \E is the ESCAPE character, and %+ %+ (that's "%+<space>%+<space>") is the cryptic description of the next two characters to send: the first to set the row, the second to set the column. The first %+ says to add the desired row number (symbolized as %, and based on the top left corner being row 0, column 0) to the ASCII value of the space character (%+). The resulting number will be taken as the ASCII value of the character that will move to the specified row. The second %+ says to do the same for the desired column.

For example, if you wanted to move to row 6, column 18 on a Wyse-50, the program would send the four character sequence "ESC=&2". The program calculates this by figuring out that the ASCII for space is 32, and 32+6=38. Thirty-eight is the ASCII value of the "&" character. Similarly, 32+18=50, which is the ASCII value of 2.

The example demonstrates the "%+" escape sequence, but there are many more escape sequences available for encoding arguments in a *termcap* file, all using the character "%". The % escapes are grouped into three classes below. The three classes are:

- % escapes that modify how later % escapes are interpreted.
- % escapes that, subject to those modifications, actually send the row or column value (encoded).

- The %% escape, which simply sends the % character.

The % argument encoding instructions in *termcap* are:

Output Operations:

%d	Send a value as a decimal number.
%2	Send a value as a two-digit decimal number.
%3	Send a value as a three-digit decimal number.
%.	Send the corresponding ASCII character value.
%+c	Add the ASCII value of character *c* to the value, and send the ASCII character that corresponds to the sum.
%%	Send a percent sign (%) literally.

Interpretation Modifiers:

%r	Reverse the order of arguments for **cm=** or **cs=**. The default is row before column, and start scrolling region before end scrolling region. %r reverses the order.
%i	Increment the values given by one. For terminals that have home based on upper left = (1,1) rather than (0,0).
%>*x,y*	If the value is greater than the ASCII value of *x*, add the ASCII value of *y* to the value. Rarely used.

Special Cases:

%n	Exclusive OR the values with 01400 before using the following % escapes to send. (DM2500 terminal.)
%B	Change the next value to binary coded decimal (((16*(*x*/10) + (*rem* (*x*/10)), where *x* is the value). (Delta Data terminal.)
%D	The next value is reverse coded (*x*-2*(*rem x*/16)), where *x* is the value. (Delta Data terminal).

Some additional examples of **cm=** are shown in the following table, with <ESC> representing the ESCAPE character. Note that the rows and columns listed are based on home = (0,0) — so an 80×24 screen actually has rows numbered 0 to 23 and columns numbered 0 to 79.

cm=	Row	Column	Chars Sent
cm=\E%d;%d	8	11	<ESC>8;11
cm=~Z%.%.	65	66	~ZAB
cm=\E%2;%2	8	11	<ESC>08;11
cm=\E%r%2;%2	8	11	<ESC>11;08
cm=\E%i%r%2;%3	8	11	<ESC>12;009
cm=\E%i%d;%d%%	8	11	<ESC>9;12%
cm=~Z%+@~Z%+@	8	11	~ZHK

Of course, your job is not to figure out the sequence that is sent given the capability description, but rather to figure out how to write the capability description when you are given its verbal description in the terminal manual. The key is to understand the description in the manual before you try to convert it to % escapes. For example, when you are writing the **cm=** capability, first find out what should be sent to move to a given spot, and then test it using the methods described in Chapter 5.

Once you understand what sequence should be sent, you can concentrate on encoding that knowledge with the correct escapes. If you are a C programmer, you can test your finished **cm=** capability with the tgoto() function in the *termcap* library. tgoto() takes a **cm=** string, a line, and a column, and generates the command string to move the cursor there. See the description of tgoto() in Appendix B.

Parameters in Terminfo

The *terminfo* description for cursor movement reads:

```
cup=\E=%p1%'\s'%+%c%p2%'\s'%+%c,
```

This is much more complicated than *termcap* on the surface, but it comes out to the same sequence of characters as in the *termcap* example. Like *termcap*, the *terminfo* argument encoding scheme is based on the "%" escape character, but provides much more flexibility.

The heart of the *terminfo* system is a stack that you can manipulate like a Reverse Polish Notation calculator. The style is thus that arguments or constants are pushed onto the stack, manipulated and combined, and a single final result (or several partial results) is output.

In the Wyse-50 example, the ESC= string is sent, and then:

%p1   says to push the first parameter onto the stack.

%'\s'   says to push a space onto the stack.

%+   says to pop the first two values on the stack, add them, and push the sum back onto the stack.

%c   says to pop the value on top of the stack as an ASCII character. This value is sent to the terminal.

To get the column specification, %p2 says to push the second parameter onto the stack, and the same sequence repeats.

Stack Operations

Like *termcap*, the special operations for handling values and manipulating the stack begin with the character "%". In all operators below which take two operands, push the leftmost operand first. For example, to subtract 5 from the first parameter, one would say %p1%{5}%-. This says to push the first parameter, and then push the number 5. Then "%-" says to pop the top two values (the first parameter and 5), subtract the second from the first, and push the difference.

Output Operations:

%%	Output the "%" character literally.
%c	Pop top of stack as an ASCII character.
%*format*	Pop the topmost value and output as specified by *format*. *format* follows the format used by the printf() function, consisting of:

– Optional flags, with the following values:

:-	Left justify, pad on right. (The colon is used to differentiate from the %- escape.)
+	Always produce a sign.
#	Use variant of main conversion operation.
<space>	Always produce either "-" sign or a space.

– An optional field width. The value popped is padded with spaces to the field width.
– An optional precision, preceded by a period, specifying the minimum number of digits to appear or, for a string, the maximum length of the string.
– A mandatory conversion character, one of:

d	Pop the value as a signed decimal number.
o	Pop the value as an unsigned octal number.
x	Pop the value as an hexadecimal number, using lower case letters **abcdef**.
X	Pop the value as an hexadecimal number, using upper case letters **ABCDEF**.
s	Pop the value as a string.

Pushing Data Onto the Stack

%p_n_   Push the _n_th parameter onto the stack. _n_ is in the range 1 to 9.
%_c_   Push character constant _c_ onto the stack.
%{_nn_**}**   Push decimal constant _nn_ onto the stack.
%l   Pop the top of the stack and push the its string length.

Using Stack Variables

%P_c_   Pop the top of the stack and set it to variable _c_. _c_ must be in the range **a** to **z** or **A** to **Z**.
%g_c_   Get variable _c_ and push it onto the stack. _c_ must be in the range **a** to **z** or **A** to **Z**.

Arithmetic Operations:

%+   Pop the top two values, add, and push the sum.
%−   Pop the top two values, subtract the second from the first, and push the result.
%*   Pop the top two values, multiply, and push the product.
%/   Pop the top two values, divide the first from the second, and push the result.
%m   Pop the top two values, modulo (2nd,1st), and push the result.

Bitwise Operations:

%&   Pop the top two values, perform a bitwise AND (2nd & 1st), and push the result.
%| Pop the top two values, perform a bitwise OR (2nd | 1st), and push the result.
%^   Pop the top two values, perform a bitwise XOR (2nd ^ 1st), and push the result.

Logical Operations:

%=   Pop the top two values and push TRUE if they are equal, FALSE if they are not.
%>   Pop the top two values and push TRUE if the second is greater than the first, FALSE otherwise.
%<   Pop the top two values and push TRUE if the second is less than the first, FALSE otherwise.
%A   Pop the top two values and push TRUE if both are true, FALSE otherwise.

%O   Pop the top two values and push TRUE if either is true, FALSE if both are false.

Unary Operations:

%!   Pop the top value and push its negation.
%~   Pop the top value and push its two's complement.

Miscellaneous Operations:

%i   Increment the values given by one. For terminals that have home based on upper left = (1,1) rather than (0,0).

%? *expr*   %t *op1* [%e *op2*] %;
            Execute *op1* if *expr* is TRUE, else execute *op2*.

Let's take the same examples we used for *termcap* parameterization and see how the equivalent *cup=* parameter string would read:

cup=	Row	Col	Chars Sent
cup=\E%p1%d;%p2%d	8	11	<ESC>8;11
cup=~Z%p1%c%p2%c	65	66	~ZAB
cup=\E%p1%2.2d;%p2%2.2d	8	11	<ESC>08;11
cup=\E%p2%2.2d;%p1%2.2d	8	11	<ESC>11;08
cup=\E%i%p2%2.2d;%p1%3.3d	8	11	<ESC>12;009
cup=\E%i%p1%d;%p2%d%%	8	11	<ESC>9;12%
cup=~Z%p1%'@'%+%c%p1%'@'%+%c	8	11	~ZHK

Encoding Examples (Termcap and Terminfo)

X Terminal windows interpret "home" as (1,1). To move the cursor to a given position, they expect an ESCAPE character followed by a square left bracket, the first argument, a semicolon, the second argument, and a capital H. The *cup=* capability definition in *terminfo* for *xterm* is:

```
cup=\E[%i%p1%d;%p2%dH
```

The **cm=** capability definition in *termcap* for *xterm* is:

```
cm=\E[%i%d;%dH
```

As a more complex example, the AT&T System V documentation discusses the Hewlett-Packard 2645, which sends the column before the row, and sends each number as a zero-padded 2-digit number. It also requires 6 milliseconds of padding. For example, to go to row 8 and column 45, the terminal needs to be sent <ESC>&a45c08Y padded for 6 milliseconds. Thus, its *terminfo* *cup=* capability is defined:

```
cup=\E&a%p2%2.2dc%p1%2.2dY$<6>
```

Its equivalent *termcap* **cm=** capability reads:

```
cm=6\E&a%r%2c%2Y
```

Terminals that used "%c" need to have the *cubl=* and *cuul=* capabilities to backspace the cursor and to move the cursor up one line. This is necessary because the system may alter or discard \n, ^D, and \r. \t can be sent because the library routines used by *terminfo* set tty modes so that tabs are never expanded. Sending \t is necessary for some terminals, notably for the Ann Arbor 4080.

Commenting Out Capabilities (Terminfo Only)

In *terminfo*, capabilities can be commented out of the sources file by preceding them with a period. For example:

```
.pad=^X,
```

Such capabilities are ignored by *tic* when it compiles the sources database. Commenting out capabilities is useful when preparing a new terminal entry.

Introduction

Reading Termcap
and Terminfo Entries

More Termcap and
Terminfo Syntax

Termcap, Terminfo
and the Shell

Writing Termcap and
Terminfo Entries

Converting Between
Termcap and Terminfo

4

Termcap, Terminfo and the Shell

Environment Variables
Default Terminal Type Specification
Setting TERM with tset
Initializing the Terminal with tset
Initializing the Terminal with tput
Using Terminfo Capabilities in Shell Programs

Before we describe more on writing *termcap* and *terminfo* entries, it is worthwhile to take a further look at how they are used. This information is essential for users and budding system administrators trying to understand why things work the way they do and, more importantly, why they sometimes do not work the way you expect. This information will also come in handy for those creating terminal entries, since it provides a foundation for testing a new entry.

This chapter is mostly about the *tset* program, which provides an efficient mechanism for assigning terminal types in your environment. *terminfo* systems do not have an analogous mechanism for determining your terminal type, but the *tput* program may be used to override the value of the TERM environment variable and to initialize your terminal at startup. The *tput* program is discussed at the end of this chapter.

Environment Variables

The TERM environment variable should be set to the user's terminal type. Upon startup of a program which uses *termcap* or *terminfo*, the program consults the value of TERM, and then searches for the specified terminal either in the */etc/termcap* or in the subdirectories of */usr/lib/terminfo*.

The TERM environment variable is usually set when the user logs in, by commands contained in the *.profile* (Bourne shell) or *.login* (C shell) file.

The variable *can* be set explicitly as described in Chapter 2, if a user always logs in on the same terminal. For example, in the Bourne shell:

```
TERM=wy50; export TERM
```

and in the C shell:

```
setenv TERM wy50
```

If the user might log in on more than one type of terminal, he or she could be prompted to enter the terminal type. The value entered could then be read into the TERM variable.

There is an optional second variable (either TERMCAP or TERMINFO) that points to the location of an alternate terminal database. The TERMCAP (or TERMINFO) variable need not be set, since if it does not exist, programs will look in the default location: that is, in */etc/termcap* or in the file */usr/lib/terminfo/?/$TERM*.

However, it is worthwhile to know that they *can* be set if desired. This is particularly useful when you are writing new entries, since you can specify another filename (TERMCAP) or directory (TERMINFO) of your choice, which contains the entry under development. If the first character of the TERMCAP variable is a slash, the variable is interpreted as a filename. For example, if you were writing a new entry for a hypothetical "bigshot" terminal, you could say:

```
$ TERMCAP=/usr/fred/bigshot; export TERMCAP (Bourne shell)
```

or:

```
% setenv TERMCAP /usr/fred/bigshot          (C shell)
```

In the case of *terminfo*, the TERMINFO variable must point to a directory containing compiled *terminfo* files, not a source file.

With *termcap*, there is one other option: the TERMCAP variable can contain the actual text of the *termcap* entry. A program called *tset*, described later in this chapter, can be used to extract the entry and place it in the environment. This speeds the startup of programs that use *termcap*, since they no longer have to search through the *termcap* file for the relevant entry: it is already right at hand. If the TERMCAP variable exists, and does not begin with a slash, it is assumed to contain an actual terminal entry, rather than a pointer to a *termcap* file.

Resetting the value of the TERMCAP or TERMINFO environment variable is useful for testing entries, when you do not want to write your entry into the system files until you know it is correct. Programs such as *tic* and *infocmp* automatically retrieve and place files in a directory hierarchy under */usr/lib/terminfo* unless the TERMINFO variable is set. If you want to use the contents of a file in another location, set the TERMINFO environment variable to point to that directory. For example:

```
$ ls /usr/tim/terminals
w
$ ls /usr/tim/terminals/w
wy50
wt50
wyse50
$ TERMINFO=/usr/tim/terminals;export TERMINFO
$ infocmp -I wy50
    ...
```

See the section "Using Environment Variables While Testing" in Chapter 5 for more information.

Default Terminal Type Specification

On systems using *termcap*, a general mechanism has evolved which involves the use of several different files and commands. To get a full picture of how it works, consider the following facilities:

* The most likely terminal type for a given serial line is "hardcoded" in the file */etc/ttytype* (many UNIX systems) or */etc/ttys* (BSD 4.3).

* If a given serial line is connected to a network, a switch, or a dialup modem, such that any number of different terminals might end up being connected to that line, that line is given a generic identifier such as *network*, *switch* or *dialup*.

* A terminal initialization program (*tset* on systems supporting *termcap*) can be used to actually set the value of TERM, as well as to perform terminal initialization once the value is set.

tset is quite complex: it can query the user for the desired terminal type; it can query the *ttytype*, *ttys*, or *inittab* file for the default terminal type; or it can perform a number of different tests to select a terminal type based on criteria such as line speed.

Before going in detail into the operation of *tset*, let's look briefly at the format of the various files in which default terminal types can be set.

The /etc/ttytype File

Most UNIX systems (including Xenix, SunOS, BSD systems through 4.2, and Version 7-derived systems) have a file called */etc/ttytype*, which allows you to associate a default terminal type with a particular serial line.

Each line in the file specifies a terminal type, followed by a tab or spaces, and the name of the special file associated with the serial line. For example:

```
vt100      tty000
wy50       tty001
```

The /etc/ttys File (BSD 4.3)

In BSD 4.3, the format of the */etc/ttys* file, which specifies whether or not a serial line is to support user logins, was changed to allow specification of additional information, including the default terminal type. The */etc/ttytype* file was done away with.

The format of the BSD 4.3 */etc/ttys* is as follows:

---
ttys Format

(BSD 4.3)

BSD 4.3 /etc/ttys

```
devname                    terminal type    comment
   |                            |              |
ttyd0 "/etc/getty std.9600" vt100 on #Tim's terminal
   |                            |
command                       status
```

In the context of this book, only the third field is significant. It contains the name of the terminal attached to the line. This should be the name as defined in the */etc/termcap* terminal database. The following additional keywords are provided to handle three cases in which a number of different terminals might end up logging in on the same line:

dialup   This line is connected to a modem.

plugboard This line is connected to a board which allows different terminal cables to be swapped.

network   This line is a local area network connection.

Note that the presence of the terminal type field in the BSD 4.3 *ttys* replaces the */etc/ttytype* file that was used for this purpose in earlier BSD versions. See a general book on UNIX system administration for more information on the use of the other fields.

In the discussion of *tset* later in this chapter, we will mention only the */etc/ttytype* file. However, if you are using BSD 4.3, please interpret these references to mean */etc/ttys*.

Setting TERM with tset

The *tset* program performs two major functions, one of which is to set the terminal type. The other is to initialize or reset the terminal. This command can be very confusing to both new users and new system administrators, not only because of its complexity, but because the two functions overlap in some non-obvious ways.

The manual page for *tset* tends to lump its two functions together, which is reasonable, considering that both are usually performed together. However, this makes it considerably more difficult to understand. For this reason, we will look at them separately.

How tset Determines the Terminal Type

In order to initialize the terminal, *tset* needs to find out the terminal type, so that it can look up the initialization string, if any, from */etc/termcap*. Because it is quite good at determining the proper type, even when TERM is not set, *tset* is also used to *set* the terminal type.

Unlike most other UNIX programs that need to know the terminal type, *tset* does not always rely on the value of TERM:

- If no arguments are specified and TERM is already set, *tset* uses the value of TERM to determine the terminal type.

- If no arguments are specified and TERM is *not* set, then *tset* uses the value specified in */etc/ttytype* or */etc/ttys* (BSD 4.3 only).

- If a terminal type is specified as an argument, that argument is used as the terminal type, regardless of the value of TERM.

- The *-m* (*map*) option allows a fine degree of control in cases where the terminal type may be ambiguous. For example, if the user sometimes logs in on a dialup line, sometimes over a local area network, and sometimes on a hardwired line, the *-m* option can be specified to determine which is currently being used, and the user can act accordingly.

It is at this point that things begin to get complex. While the *-m* option could be used to determine the terminal type for purposes of resetting the terminal, it is really the sort of thing that gets built into a login file and forgotten. It is really most useful when combined with other options that not only query the terminal type but actually set it. So let's jump ahead to look at how that is done.

Telling It to the Shell

Because it has been designed so cleverly to find out the terminal type by prompting the user, or mapping generic entries in the */etc/ttytype* file, *tset* can also be used in a *.profile* or *.login* file to set the value of TERM.

Given the – option, *tset* prints the value that it determines for the terminal type to standard output. TERM can thus be set in the Bourne shell as follows:

```
TERM=`tset - -Q options`; export TERM
```

(The *-Q* (*quiet*) option causes *tset* to suppress printing of a message it normally prints regarding the values to which it has set the Erase and Kill characters—a job it does in its alternate role as terminal initializer. The backquotes surrounding the *tset* command cause its output to be interpolated into the command line.)

For C shell users, *tset* has an even more powerful function. The *-s* option causes it to send to standard output a series of C shell commands not only to set TERM, but also to set the TERMCAP variable to the actual contents of the *termcap* entry. This speeds up launch time for programs that use *termcap*: they no longer need to search through the *termcap* file until they find the relevant entry; it is already at hand.

To actually have the commands executed rather than printed to the screen, you should invoke *tset* as follows:

```
set noglob
eval `tset -Q -s [options]`
unset noglob
```

The *eval* command causes the *tset* output to be executed within the shell. (Although *tset* has a *set noglob* and *unset noglob* built into its output, the C shell does not properly interpret them so they have to executed by hand.)

In order to understand what *tset* is doing, let's take a moment to send its output to the screen (i.e., issue the command without evaluating it):

```
% tset -Q -s wy50
set noglob;
setenv TERM wy50 ;
setenv TERMCAP 'n9|wy50:li#24:co#80:am:bs:bw:ul:\
:cm=\E=%+\040%+\040:nd=^L:up=^K:do=^J:ho=^^:bt=\EI:\
:cl=^Z:ce=\ET:cd=\EY:al=\EE:dl=\ER:ic=\EQ:dc=\EW:\
:so=\EG4:se=\EG0:sg#1:ue=\EG0:us=\EG8:ug#1\040:\
:me=\E(EG0:mb=\EG2:mp=\E):mh=\EGp:mr=\EG4:mk=\EG1:\
:kl=^H:kr=^L:ku=^K:kd=^J:kh=^^:k1=^A@^M:k2=^AA^M:\
:k3=^AB^M:k4=^AC^M:k5=^AD^M:k6=^AE^M:k7=^AF^M:k8=^AG^M:\
:k9=^AH^M:k0=^AI^M' ;
unset noglob;
```

The *set noglob* command causes the shell to suspend interpretation of special characters; otherwise the presence of these characters in the *termcap* entry could cause problems. After execution, the shell is reset to its normal state.

The use of *tset* to set the TERMCAP environment variable can cause problems for new users who do not understand it completely. For example, as long as the TERMCAP variable is not set, programs look by default in */etc/termcap*. However, once the TERMCAP variable contains the actual *termcap* entry, changing the value of TERM will no longer have any effect on a program like *vi*.

If you set the value of TERM correctly but *vi* still does not seem to work, check to make sure that TERMCAP is not still set to the actual *termcap* entry. You can clear this condition with the command:

    % **unsetenv TERMCAP**   *(C shell)*

or:

    $ **TERMCAP=**   *(Bourne shell)*

or:

    $ **unset TERMCAP**   *(newer Bourne shells)*

Tset Examples

Now let's look at some examples of how *tset* works. While *tset* is generally invoked from within the *.profile* or *.login* file, we will give some examples from the command line, since they make it more explicit what the command is actually doing. First, our assumptions:

```
% tty
/dev/tty000
% echo $TERM
TERM: Undefined variable
% grep tty000 /etc/ttytype
vt100     tty000
```

The user is logged in on */dev/tty000*; the value of TERM is undefined; and the */etc/ttytype* file says that a vt100 terminal is connected to */dev/tty000*. Furthermore, let's say that a Wyse-50 is actually connected to that line.

For purposes of example, we do not want to actually set the terminal type but simply demonstrate which terminal type *tset* will select. Accordingly, we will use the – option to print the terminal type selected to standard output. *tset* will also try to initialize the terminal, which may cause problems if the terminal type is specified incorrectly.

The command:

```
$ tset - -Q
vt100
```

will attempt to initialize the terminal by sending out a vt100 initialization string. Since this is actually a Wyse-50, some stray escape characters will pop out on the screen, garbling what is there and failing miserably to reset the terminal.

To get *tset* to initialize the terminal properly, we could do several things:

- If a Wyse-50 is permanently connected to this serial line, we could (and should) correct the entry in */etc/ttytype*.
- We could simply set the value of TERM:

```
$ TERM=wy50; tset - -Q
wy50
```

- We could specify the terminal type as an argument:

```
$ tset - -Q wy50
wy50
```

Now, let's consider a more complex case, in which the serial line is connected to a dialup modem, through which several different users might be connected, each using a different type of terminal. Accordingly, the default terminal type in */etc/ttytype* should be set to *dialup*. The *tset* command could then be used in the *.profile* or in the *.login* file as follows:

```
eval 'tset -s -Q -m 'dialup:adm3a' '
```

This means that if *ttytype* says *dialup*, use *adm3a* as the terminal type. A colon separates the *ttytype* value and the value to which it is to be mapped. If you want the user to be prompted to be sure, place a question mark after the colon and before the mapped terminal type:

```
eval 'tset -s -Q -m 'dialup:?adm3a' '
TERM = (adm3a)
```

If the user presses RETURN, the preferred terminal type will be used. Alternatively, another terminal type could be entered at that time.

You can cause *tset* to prompt for a terminal type even without testing a generic entry like dialup. Let's demonstrate this on the command line:

```
$ tset -Q -m "?adm3a"
TERM = (adm3a)
```

It is also possible to specify different terminal types for different line speeds. Say, for example, that you normally used a Wyse-50 with a 2400 bps modem when dialing in from home, but used a portable PC with a vt100 terminal emulator and 1200 bps modem when you were on the road. You might then use a *tset* command like this:

```
eval 'tset -s -Q -m 'dialup@1200:vt100' wy50'
```

Assuming that the type is set in *ttytype* as *dialup*, *tset* will use the type *vt100* if at 1200 bps and, if not, will use the type *wy50*.

Various symbols can be used for line speed calculations: *>speed* means greater than the specified speed; *<speed* means less than the specified speed; *@speed* means at the specified speed. An exclamation point can precede the operator to reverse the sense of the comparison. (For example, !@1200 would mean at any speed other than 1200 bps.)*

Multiple *-m* options can be specified; the first map to be satisfied will be used. If no match is found, a final value specified on the line without a *-m* option (as in the above example) will be used. If no value is specified, the type in */etc/ttytype* will be used.

Initializing the Terminal with tset

The proper function of *tset* is actually to initialize the terminal. It outputs an initialization string (if one is defined in the terminal's *termcap* entry), which should set the terminal to a reasonable state. In this role, it overlaps somewhat with *stty*, setting the erase and kill characters to ^H and ^X. (Options allow the user to specify alternate values for these characters, as well as for the interrupt character.) When done, it prints the following message:

```
Erase is control-H
Kill is control-X
```

(or whatever else you have set these characters to). As mentioned earlier, this message can be suppressed by adding the *-Q* (*quiet*) option.

A special form of the *tset* command, called *reset*, is found on some systems. In addition to *tset*'s normal processing, it sets various *stty* modes to what it considers a "reasonable" state. It can thus be used to reset both the terminal and the serial line control parameters in cases where a bombing program or user bungling has left the terminal in an unusable state.

---

* Watch out for line speed switches. They don't work on a lot of networked systems—usually, the line speed at the computer's port is higher than the speed of the terminal.

There are some cases in which normal end-of-line processing has been disabled, and the system will no longer perform the carriage-return to line-feed translation UNIX requires to work with most terminals. In these cases, you may need to type:

```
^Jreset^J
```

to get *reset* to work.

The *stty sane* command can also be used to restore terminals from a "corrupted" state:

```
^Jstty sane^J
```

Initializing the Terminal with tput

The *tput* program used with *terminfo* is somewhat equivalent to *tset*, but does not have the ability that *tset* has to determine the terminal type. On the other hand, it allows you to pick out particular terminal capabilities and print out their values or store them into shell variables. This allows shell programs to make use of terminal capabilities such as inverse video or underlining.

By default, *tput* assumes that you are using the terminal type specified by the TERM variable. If you want to override the value of TERM, you can specify another terminal type with the -*T* option. For example:

```
$ tput -Twy50 ...
```

In System V Release 3, *tput* has a keyword option that allows you to reset the terminal by outputting the initialization strings (there are several) from a *terminfo* description:

```
$ tput init
```

The command:

```
$ tput reset
```

issues the reset strings from the *terminfo* entry. If no reset strings are defined, the initialization strings are issued instead, and the command acts exactly like *tput init*.

In earlier releases of System V, these keywords are not supported, and you must issue multiple *tput* commands to output each of the initialization or reset strings by name.

The following shell program, contributed by Tony Hansen of AT&T, will do the trick:

```
:
# Evaluate and output the iprog capability
eval `tput iprog`
# output the is1 and is2 initialization strings
tput is1
tput is2

# if the terminal supports tabs, set them
# otherwise, disable them
if [ -n "`tput ht`" ]
then stty tabs; tabs -8
else stty -tabs
fi
# output contents of the initialization file, if present
cat -s "`tput if`"
# output the is3 initialization string
tput is3
```

See Chapter 10 for a description of the various initialization capabilities used in this script.

Using Terminfo Capabilities in Shell Programs

The ability of *tput* to print out the value of any individual capability makes it possible to use terminal capabilities such as those for standout mode in shell programs.

For example, a prompt issued by a shell program could be highlighted by the following code:

```
# Store the terminfo capability to start standout mode into
# the variable HIGHLIGHT
HIGHLIGHT=`tput smso`
# Store the terminfo capability to end standout mode into
# the variable NORMAL
NORMAL=`tput rmso`
# Echo a highlighted prompt
echo "${HIGHLIGHT}Press Return to accept value: ${NORMAL}\c"
```

In System V Release 3, capabilities that accept arguments (such as cursor movement sequences) will interpolate values that follow the capability name on the command line. For example, to issue the cursor motion sequence to move to the top left corner of the screen (row 0, column 0), you could type:

```
$ tput cup 0 0
```

Another case where *tput* comes in useful is when command sequences accidentally get sent to the screen, leaving output garbled or in a distracting highlight mode. It sometimes happens that a user reads a non-ASCII file, or reads a mail message with a control character accidentally imbedded, and ends up with gibberish. This is often because the sequence for entering an alternate character set has been sent to the terminal, and the screen is no longer readable to the human eye. The user can return to the normal character set two ways: by rebooting the terminal, or by entering *tput rmacs* on the command line. Using *tput*, obviously, is much more efficient.

For more information, see the manual page *tput(1)*.

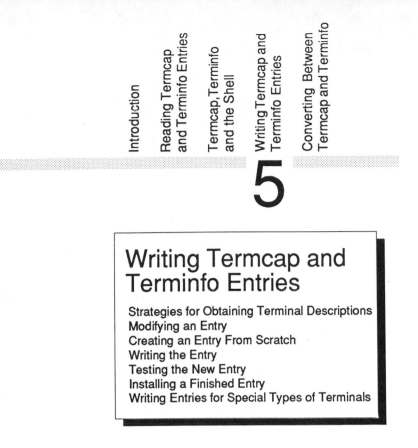

5

Writing Termcap and Terminfo Entries

Strategies for Obtaining Terminal Descriptions
Modifying an Entry
Creating an Entry From Scratch
Writing the Entry
Testing the New Entry
Installing a Finished Entry
Writing Entries for Special Types of Terminals

This chapter describes how to write a *termcap* or *terminfo* entry. It contains suggestions on strategy (is it better to try to obtain the entry from another site, modify an existing entry, or write from scratch?), techniques for determining what capabilities a terminal has (besides reading the terminal manual!), and examples of some particular types of entry you might need to create.

It should be useful to system managers and programmers who want to:

• Modify an existing entry.

• Prepare a new entry.

• Debug an entry that is causing problems.

If anything in this chapter does not make sense, press on and read Part 2, which describes in more detail all the existing capabilities; then reread this chapter.

Strategies for Obtaining Terminal Descriptions

All right. You've bought a new terminal, hooked it up, and discovered that your system doesn't have a *termcap* or *terminfo* entry for it. Or maybe you've heard about a new terminal at an attractive price, and you'd like to switch your buying patterns.

You can create a new entry from scratch, working from the terminal manual and experimenting on the terminal itself. We'll describe in detail how to do this later in this chapter. But first, let's look at some alternatives that may save you time and effort.

The easiest alternative is to get someone else to write the entry for you—or, rather, to find someone who has already had to do it. We will point you to several good sources for terminal descriptions.

If that fails, you may be able to find an entry for a similar terminal that you can modify. This is especially likely when a new terminal is one in a family, when the terminal is a cheaper "look-alike" version of an existing terminal, or when the terminal has an emulation mode that makes it work like an established terminal. (In all of these cases, the emulation may not be 100 percent accurate.)

Obtaining an Entry

The very best method for obtaining an entry from another site is to post a request to Usenet, the international network of UNIX systems.

Usenet is something like the electronic bulletin boards common in the PC world but is distributed among thousands of systems. It includes one newsgroup, called *comp.terminals*, that is reserved for postings of terminal descriptions and discussion of terminal features. If your site is connected to Usenet, you can read the contents of this group by typing the command:

```
$ readnews -n comp.terminals
```

Because the volume of Usenet news is so great, only a few weeks worth of postings (at most) will probably be available on line. However, your system's Usenet administrator may have archived past news traffic; if so, you might want to restore and scan through previous messages. (If not, it is possible that a neighboring site keeps complete archives and can be persuaded to search them for you.)

If no description turns up, you can post a message requesting help with the *postnews* program. Here is an example of the terminal dialogue involved in posting a news article requesting help.

```
$ postnews
Is this message in response to any other message? n
Subject: Looking for Wyse-60 termcap description
Keywords: termcap, wy60, help!
Newsgroups (enter one at a time, end with a blank line).

The most relevant newsgroup should be the first.  You
should add others only if your article really MUST be read
by people who choose not to read the appropriate group for
your article.  But DO use multiple newsgroups rather than
posting many times.

For a list of newsgroups, type ?
> comp.terminals
>
```

Terminate the list of newsgroups by pressing RETURN at the > prompt. You will be placed in *vi* (or possibly another editor such as *emacs* if it is in more common use at your site) and can compose your message. If you end up in an editor you are not familiar with, then set the environment variable EDITOR to the name of your favorite editor; when you reinvoke postnews, it will use that editor instead. Note that you will need to use a terminal that has a working *termcap* or *terminfo* entry in order to use a visual editor such as *vi* or *emacs*. Keep your message short and to the point. Include a request for the *termcap* description to be mailed to you instead of being posted. When you write the file and quit, you will be prompted:

```
What now? [send, edit, list, quit, write]
```

Type s to post your message. You should see the message:

```
Article posted successfully
```

You may receive replies by mail, or replies may be posted to the news-group. You should continue to read the group for a couple of weeks or until you get the response you want.

See the Nutshell Handbooks *Managing UUCP and Usenet* and *Using UUCP and Usenet* for more information on how to connect to Usenet (including sites where you can gain temporary access if your own system is not connected).

Other Sources of Terminal Descriptions

If you are not connected to Usenet, don't despair. There are still a number of sources through which you might be able to find an entry prepared for your terminal.

You are looking either for a UNIX user who bought the same terminal and had to create an entry for it or for someone with a different UNIX system which was distributed with an entry for *wy60* in their */etc/termcap* or *terminfo* file hierarchy.

Another place to try is the dealership from which you bought your terminal. While they probably do not have an entry waiting on the shelf, they are a good source for leads. They might be able to put you in contact with other customers who have a UNIX system like yours who would have been faced with the same problem.

(Warning: all terminal descriptions are not created equal. The entries vary greatly in quality. Consider, the entry you create may be taken and modified by someone else, and so on again and again. The nature of *termcap* and *terminfo* is such that errors can lie hidden until a given capability is used, and even then the error may not be apparent or the user might not pursue a little glitch. Company-supplied entries are no more guaranteed than individually created entries. Testing the entry is key. Use it, put it through its paces. If possible, compare the entry to another for any discrepancies. See later in this chapter for information on testing entries.)

Modifying an Entry

If you cannot find an entry that matches your new terminal, you will have to either write the entry from scratch or find an entry for a similar terminal that you can modify. Naturally, it is easier to modify an existing entry, since you will have something to work with.

Equivalent Terminals

Some terminals closely resemble other terminals: this happens because a manufacturer wants to maintain consistency across a product line or to create a "look-alike" terminal that can emulate a more expensive make.

In addition, some terminals have many possible enhancement boards or switches that you would not change at run time. These options make the terminal look like a similar, but slightly changed, terminal. An entry in the */etc/termcap* file or */usr/lib/terminfo* file hierarchy is required for each of the options that you want to support. Usually these entries will be identical in all but a few capabilities. For example, the Digital Equipment Corporation *vt100* can run in 80 or 132 column mode. Separate entries need to be available for both modes.

You must distinguish between "setup options" that require their own entry, and "run time options" (such as switching to standout mode) that do not need a different entry. Sometimes the difference is not clear. Some setup options do not require any hardware changes but are generated by the user via a setup menu. Do not create a different entry for each possible change in the setup menu!

Block cursor vs. underline cursor, key click vs. silent—these are setup options that do not change how the terminal looks to a program. However, changing the screen width (as on the *vt100*) is a run time option that does affect the fundamental layout of the screen; it merits two separate but similar entries.

There is one other use for equivalent terminals: if you have any terminals that do not have good entries, you can create an extremely simple terminal type, one with only the most basic capabilities (like the Lear

Siegler ADM-3a), and give it the terminal name "temp." You can use this simple entry until you have something better. That allows you to run (or at least walk) your new terminal

If two terminals are substantially similar (for example, a vt100 in 80- or 132-column mode) it may be appropriate to use the equivalent terminal capability rather than writing a completely new entry. The *termcap* **tc=** or *terminfo* **use=** capability allows you to read the capabilities from one entry into another. Capabilities can then be added, deleted or changed from those of the equivalent terminal.

There are several advantages to using **tc=** (*use=*) instead of typing in all the capabilities by hand. First, it saves time and avoids the mistakes that are made when typing. Second, it is self-documenting, telling others where the entry for that terminal originated. Third, if you find that a capability in the original entry needs to be changed, it will automatically be changed in all the entries that use **tc=** to make themselves equivalent to that terminal.

This can also be a disadvantage. If the capability is right for one of the **tc=** equivalents but wrong in the original, it should not be changed in the look-alike terminal. For this reason, it is a good idea to search for all **tc=** entries when you make a change, either inside the editor or by using *grep*.

You should also document all changes you make to the original *termcap* file with comments in */etc/termcap*, just as you would with a program.

An '@' following a capability can be used to indicate that the terminal lacks a capability that the equivalent terminal has. For example, if the newline capability does not exist, it can be described as **nl@**, which negates the **nl** description. See Chapter 15 for more information on using this capability.

Comparing Entries

If you have more than one *terminfo* entry for a given terminal, you can compare them using *infocmp*, as described at the end of Chapter 6. A shell script that can be helpful in comparing *termcap* entries is also shown in Chapter 6.

Creating an Entry From Scratch

Writing and debugging a new entry is more art than science, just like all programming. There is no formula, but there are methods for learning and testing a terminal's capabilities. Steps in designing an entry include:

- Read the terminal manual! It should describe the special features of the terminal and, in particular, the escape sequences and control codes that turn on and turn off special terminal modes.
- Test the capabilities of the terminal by sending control sequences manually to the terminal.
- Write (and, for *terminfo*, compile) the entry.
- Test the entry using a program like *vi* that will exercise all of the features of the terminal.
- Repeat previous steps as necessary.

Read the Manual!

The technical guide to your terminal is your bible. However, each guide is different, and some are much easier to use than others. They usually start with an overview of the terminal, describing the features that are sure to make it the industry standard. This helps get you oriented to the terminal and points out special features that may well need a capability. Be sure to reread such a general description section after you have created your entry, to be sure that you are not letting a special feature go to waste.

The other important section in such a guide will be a table of special control codes for the terminal. This is the source of information for all string capabilities. These tables are organized in some sort of alphabetical order, maybe starting with the effects of the CONTROL characters from ^A to ^Z, then the ESCAPE characters, then CONTROL-ESCAPE characters, and so on. The string capabilities in which you are interested will be buried somewhere in this table.

You should first know what you are looking for, so make sure you are familiar with all the capabilities listed in Part 2 of this handbook. Then follow this procedure for transferring information from the manual to your prototype entry:

1. Go through the table of control strings and highlight the ones that seem to correspond to a *termcap* or *terminfo* string capability.

2. Examine each of the capabilities that you highlighted so that you understand its function.

3. Make a list of these capabilities on a separate sheet of paper.

4. Use an editor to write the new entry in a separate file in one of your own directories.

Your terminal handbook will also describe how to set up the terminal, both physically and with software options. Many of these options set communication parameters like baud rate, handshake protocols, and parity. Obviously, you must set up your terminal correctly, and it helps to be fluent with all the software setup modes.

However, most of this information is not specified in a capability. (Options like automatic newline on carriage return and wraparound are exceptions, since they do have corresponding Boolean capabilities.) As you read about these options, keep in mind how they might affect your entry, but pay most attention to learning how to set up and manipulate your terminal.

Exercise the Terminal

If you cannot find the terminal manual, order a new one from the terminal manufacturer; doing so will save you hours of time and effort.

However, if you only want to modify an existing entry, or if the manual does not seem to tell you everything you want to know, you may be able to find out some of what you know by experimenting with the terminal. In particular, you should be able to find out what character strings any of the special keys on the keyboard send.

Even if you have the manual, and it is complete, it may well be worthwhile to make sure that you understand all of the control sequences by testing them on the terminal. Testing assures you that you understand the format of the command, lets you see what the command actually does, and may bring out relationships between commands and setup options that are not initially apparent.

In addition, some capabilities may not be documented in your manual. For example, you can only find out if your terminal can move the cursor gracefully to an absolute location while in highlight mode (some terminals can't) by testing.

Finding Out What Special Keys Send

If you are working without a terminal manual, start by trying to find out what characters are generated by labeled keys like arrows, HOME, BACKSPACE, CLEAR, and Function Keys.

This information is useful for specifying both a key definition capability (such as **kC=** *(termcap)*, or *kclr=* *(terminfo)* the sequence sent by the CLEAR key) and the equivalent command capability (such as **cl=(termcap)**, or *clear=* **(terminfo)**the command to clear the screen). (See the section "Other Special Keyboard Keys" in Chapter 12 for a discussion of the difference between these two related sets of capabilities.)

For example, if you find out that the CLEAR key sends ^Z, you can then specify:

```
:cl=^Z:kC=^Z:        (termcap)
clear=^Z, kclr=^Z,   (terminfo)
```

There are a several on-line techniques for finding out what character is sent by a special key. Each has drawbacks, but between them, you can almost always find out what character a key generates.

- Enter insert mode in *vi*, and use the ^V control sequence to quote each special key. That is, type CTRL-V, followed by the key whose identity you are trying to discover. A printable representation of the key should appear on the screen.

  This will not work if the key generates a sequence containing more than one non-printing character, since ^V will only quote the first one. It also will not work for keys that generate a newline (such as the down-arrow key on the Wyse-50 keyboard)—but in such a case, the action of the key should be obvious.

- At the command line, print:

  ```
  $ stty -echo; cat -v; stty echo
  ```

  and then type the special keys, each followed by a carriage return. *cat* will echo the translated version on the screen. When you are finished, type CTRL-D.

- Simply type the special key at the shell prompt. As long as the key does not have meaning to the shell (e.g., ^C or ^D), the command generated by the key will be executed on the terminal. Depending on the version of UNIX you use, a printable equivalent to the command generated by the key you pressed may also be printed as the command is executed.* On some systems, the control character is recognized on input and is echoed in two separate ways: as a printable representation of the control character (e.g., ^Z—literally, caret-Z) and as the actual control character. Other systems echo only the actual control character, which means that you see the effect but not the character that caused it.

  In either case, the shell will give an error message containing the character typed as soon as you press the RETURN key. The message should read something like this:

  ```
  ^[[U : Command not found.
  ```

---

*Keep in mind that with full-duplex communications, characters are not sent from your keyboard directly to your terminal but are sent to the system and echoed back to the terminal.

If, on the other hand, the key generates a sequence that is meaningful to the shell, some standard function, such as interrupt, end-of-file, or suspend, will be executed. You can find out what command invokes each of these functions using *stty*(1).

Observing the Effect of a Capability

Checking capabilities on your terminal is like debugging a program. You must think of a way to make your terminal demonstrate what it does in response to a command. This can require some creativity.

Some capabilities, such as the clear screen command, are easy to check. In any mode, when your terminal is sent the control code to clear the screen, the screen should be cleared. But if you want to check, for instance, movement while in standout mode, you may need to go to greater lengths, creating a file containing the appropriate special characters (using the "^V" sequence to quote special characters), and then *catting* it to the screen.

You can use *cat* directly by collecting input from the keyboard, typing a line starting with ^D, and watching what happens when *cat* sends the input it has collected back to the terminal.

Note that the effect will be slightly different, depending on whether or not your system echoes a printable version of the control character.

As an example, consider checking the home capability which moves the cursor to the top left corner of the screen. Let us assume that your home capability is ^Z (as it is on the Wyse-50) and that you are using a system without Berkeley job control. (If you are on a system where ^Z is the suspend character, you would have to use *stty*(1) to temporarily change it to something else.) Type *cat*, some lines of text, a ^Z, some more lines of text, and then a ^D.

```
john% cat
This is a test
of this terminal's
home capability.
^ZThese two lines should print
at the top of the screen after you type Control-D.
^D
```

Typing ^D tells UNIX that you have finished entering text. *cat* will send the input back to the screen, starting from the line containing the cursor. The ^Z will cause the cursor to move to the home position (the top left) where the rest of the text will be printed.

This example assumes the first type of system, which sent the printable representation of ^Z when it was echoing the characters and sent the real ^Z when *catting* back the input after the ^D. The other type of system would have echoed back a ^Z when you press it, and the terminal would have gone to the upper lefthand corner at that time.

Beware that using *cat* directly will not work as shown on some older BSD systems. For those systems, try sending the output of *cat* to */dev/null*. On a BSD system, use the syntax:

```
% stty -ctlecho; cat >/dev/null; stty ctlecho
```

or on System V:

```
$ cat >/dev/null
```

Writing the Entry

You can create a *termcap* or *terminfo* entry with any text editor. (Of course, you will need another terminal with a correct entry in order to edit!) Refer to Chapter 2 of this book for some details on syntax.

Rather than placing the entry under development in */etc/termcap* or the */usr/lib/terminfo* directory hierarchy, you should put it in a separate file in one of your own directories. You may also want to develop the entry in stages, first writing in only essential capabilities, and adding others once you have confidence in the basic design of your entry.

Test and debug your entry until the terminal performs as it should. If you are using *terminfo*, you will need to recompile the entry with *tic* after each modification to the source file. With *termcap*, you can test the new entry as soon as the change is made.

Using Environment Variables While Testing

When testing an entry, you should reset the environment variable TERM and also either TERMCAP or TERMINFO, depending on what system you are using. As described earlier, rather than adding your unde-bugged, partially working terminal entry to the system database, put it in your personal directory. You can have multiple versions of the ter-minal description in a file, each with a slightly different name, and then switch between them by resetting the TERM variable. If you are using *termcap*, set the TERMCAP variable to the full pathname of the file; if you are using TERMINFO, remember to set the TERMINFO variable to some directory other than */usr/lib/terminfo* before running the *terminfo* compiler *tic*, or else your entry will attempt to go into the system data-base.

Compiling Terminfo Entries

terminfo entries must be compiled with *tic* (terminfo compiler) before they can be accessed with other programs. To use *tic*, simply specify as an argument the name of a file containing *terminfo* source entries. For example:

```
$ tic wy50.src
```

If a filename is not given, *terminfo.src* will be taken as the default source file.

tic will automatically create compiled entries for each of the aliases on the terminal's name line (except for the long name). They will be placed in separate files in a directory hierarchy under the directory specified by the TERMINFO variable or in */usr/lib/terminfo* if that vari-able is not set. If the directory does not exist, it will be created. The subdirectories will have single-letter names based on the first letter of the alias names specified.

For example, assuming the following alias line is found in the file */usr/tim/terminals/wy50.src* :

```
wy50|wt50|Wyse Technologies WY-50|,
```

if we run *tic* after setting the TERMINFO variable to */usr/tim/terminals*:

```
$ TERMINFO=/usr/tim/terminals; export TERMINFO
$ tic wy50.src
$ ls /usr/tim/terminals
w
$ ls /usr/tim/terminals/w
wy50
wt50
```

The subdirectory *w* was created, and the compiled entry was placed in the file *wy50*. This entry was then automatically linked to another file with the name of the second alias for the terminal, *wt50*.

You may want to run *tic* with the *-v* (*verbose*) option, which will give a running commentary on the compilation. A numeric argument will increase the level of debugging output. To have as much detail as possible, specify the option *-v9*.

Note that if there are several *terminfo* entries in the same source file, they will all be compiled.

Error Messages from tic

As will be described shortly, *termcap* entries are interpreted at run time, so *termcap* error messages occur at run time. In contrast, errors in *terminfo* entries are generally detected when the entry is compiled.

One of the important jobs of any compiler is to check its source for correct syntax. Fortunately, the System V Release 3 *tic* program is blessed with a full set of clear diagnostic messages. *tic* checks the syntax of the names and the capabilities, it warns you if it cannot build the file hierarchy, and it sometimes suggests that you might have accidentally left out a comma because a string capability is abnormally long.

The System V Release 3 documentation for *tic* lists more than 30 different messages. See the *tic*(1) manual page for the full list of messages.

Testing the New Entry

Once you have entered a complete *termcap* entry into a file or compiled a *terminfo* entry, it is time to test that the entry does the job.

Testing with vi

Because *termcap* was originally developed with *vi* in mind and because *vi* is one of the more complex programs that will need to use the entry, it is probably the best program with which to test the accuracy and completeness of your new entry.

Try out all of the cursor movement and scrolling keys (note that h, j, k, and l should always work, but that arrow keys will only work if their corresponding capabilities are defined) and add and delete lines. In particular, you should try inserting a large amount of text, then repeat the insert with "." or with the yank and put commands. (Errors while inserting large amounts of text with one of these commands may indicate the need for padding, as explained in the next section.)

Note that *vi* is a clever program, because it can run on both smart and dumb terminals. It will take advantage of terminal capabilities that let it work fast, but it can run on terminals without those capabilities.

The minimum requirements for *vi* to run in visual mode are the *termcap* capabilities **co#**, **li#**, **up=**, and **cl=** (in *terminfo*, **cols#**, **lines#**, **cup=** and **clear=**). It must know the size of the terminal, and the terminal must have commands to move the cursor up a line and to clear the screen. Everything else *vi* can live without. For example, it can simulate a backspace by doing a carriage return (without a new line) and then retyping the characters all over again until it reaches one space in front of where it started. It finds similar ways to work around other missing features. Obviously, this is highly inefficient, but it allows *vi* to work when other programs might not.

If your terminal cannot clear or go up a line, *vi* will run in open mode, which means it only works a line at a time.

If you want to see how *vi* uses the terminal capabilities to save itself some work, use the *stty*(1) command to set your serial line to a slow baud rate (say 150). Since the system and the terminal will now be out of sync, the terminal will be temporarily inoperable. Use your terminal's setup mode (or DIP switches if terminal setup is done in hardware) to set the terminal to the same baud rate.

Now, when you use *vi*, you should be able to see the order in which characters are sent. This is a good way to debug a *termcap* or *terminfo* entry.

Be aware that *vi* adjusts its strategy based on the terminal capabilities that are available, and even on the baud rate. Productive testing requires some knowledge of how *vi* is supposed to work.

What Capabilities Are Being Used?

If you are unsure what capabilities *vi* (or any program) is using to perform some operation, you can find out by creating a dummy *termcap* or *terminfo* entry. This "fake" entry will output an identifying printable string for each capability. In *termcap*, the entry might look something like this:

```
dm|dummy|test|fake entry for finding capabilities:\
    :co#24:li#80:\
    :up=iUP\E:do=iDOWN\E:le=iLEFT\E:nd=iRIGHT\E:\
    :ho=iHOME\E:ll=iLL\E:\
    :al=iADDLINE\E:\
        . . .
```

For each capability, the letter "i" is sent to place *vi* in input mode, an identifying string is output, and an Escape is output to place *vi* back in command mode. A similar entry might be made in *terminfo*. If you then set your terminal type to "dummy," every time you tell *vi* to move down a space, the string:

```
DOWN
```

will appear on the screen, telling you which capability is being used. This type of test can be adapted for any program which uses *termcap* or *terminfo*, not just *vi*.

Error Messages in Termcap

The low-level programs which access *termcap* send error messages if the *termcap* entry does not make sense. These error messages can help you debug a new entry. They do not check meaning, of course, but only the syntax and format of the fields. The error messages are:

√   **Bad termcap entry**
Syntax of entry is wrong. Check for colons and line breaks.

√   **Infinite tc= loop**
Chain of **tc=** capabilities is too long, so system assumes that there is a loop.

√   **termcap entry too long**
The *termcap* entry is too long to fit in a system dependent buffer. Make shorter by moving initialization sequence from **is=** to **if=** and by removing optional entries. Reduce length and/or number of terminal aliases.

√   **oops**
There is an error in a parameterized sequence. Check all capabilities that use parameters for proper syntax.

As described previously, *terminfo* error messages will be displayed when the entry is compiled rather than when it is used.

When to Use Padding

Some terminals need time to digest certain commands: they cannot receive further output from a program until they finish processing the current output. This extra time is called *padding*.

The amount of time a terminal takes to do a command is terminal-dependent, so there are no general rules defining which capabilities should be padded and by how much. You will have to refer to your terminal handbook for the raw numbers or perform some tests, if the terminal handbook does not supply the information. See Chapter 3 for more information on padding syntax for *termcap* and *terminfo*.

You can sometimes test your padding specifications with *vi*. Perform this test when the system is not overloaded:

1. Connect your terminal to the system at the fastest baud rate available.

2. Go into *vi* and force *vi* to use the capability you want to test.

   This may take some ingenuity. For example, to test the **al=** capability to add lines, fill the screen full of text, delete, say, 16 lines from the middle of the screen by giving the command "16dd", then give *vi* the "u" command several times quickly, forcing it to add lines and put the text back, delete them again, put them back again, etc.

3. If the screen gets garbled and characters lost, it could be because the capability had insufficient padding. Try increasing the padding, and repeat the test.

In general, specifying padding is a trial-and-error procedure. One good thing to remember is that insufficient padding may be the cause of erratic, inconsistent terminal behavior. Although it does no real harm to specify more padding for terminal capabilities than is necessary, it does slow your terminal down, so you should try your best to provide the perfect amount of padding.

Instead of padding, some terminals use the XON/XOFF flow control system. The XON/XOFF system is somewhat more efficient because the terminal stops and starts the computer from sending characters as needed, instead of always sending enough padding to handle the worst case. See Chapter 3 for a full description of XON/XOFF handling.

Installing a Finished Entry

Once you are satisfied that your terminal description works correctly, you can install it in the default system location: the */etc/termcap* file or the */usr/lib/terminfo* directory hierarchy.

The following sections provide several hints and caveats for developers of terminal descriptions.

Organizing your Termcap Entries (Termcap only)

When a program is going to use *termcap*, it must first find the entry in */etc/termcap* for the current terminal. It does this by searching through */etc/termcap* from start to finish, checking the terminal name line. Consequently, the entries for the terminals most used on your system should be copied to the start of the */etc/termcap* file. This will reduce the time it takes to look up the capabilities for those terminals.

/etc/termcap is organized by manufacturers. The entries should be copied and added to the front without deleting the originals so that the organization of */etc/termcap* by manufacturers is left intact. As always, when there are two copies of data, be careful when you modify one. A good procedure is to modify the first copy of the *termcap* entry and not the second: in this way, your terminals will use the modified version and the original version will be available as a backup. Document the change in both places.

Using an Alias Twice (Termcap only)

The positioning of entries in the */etc/termcap* file is sometimes used to choose which options of a terminal are used. For example, the Digital vt100 can be set up in a variety of modes. The names use flags to indicate which mode they are in. The -am suffix indicates automatic margins, the -nam suffix indicates no automatic margins. The following are the alias lines for two vt100 entries in a System V */etc/termcap*:

```
d0|vt100|vt100-am|dec vt100:\

d1|vt100|vt100-nam|vt100 w/no am:\
```

Both of these alias lines contain the entry "vt100". So what happens if you specify that your terminal is a "vt100"? Do you get the entry with automatic margins or the one without? The answer is you get the entry which is first in the */etc/termcap*. This */etc/termcap* uses the vt100 alias twice (violating one of the naming rules!) intentionally, allowing the local system administrator to get the version of the vt100 they prefer by putting it first, without making any other changes in the file.

This is not an endorsement of this technique, only a warning of what you might find in */etc/termcap*.

Software Updates

When you mount a new version of your system, it may have new
/etc/termcap or a new */usr/lib/terminfo* hierarchy. If so, remember to
add to it any entries you have created. Also, check the new
/etc/termcap or */usr/lib/terminfo* for new terminal entries that have been
added.

Introduction

Reading Termcap and Terminfo Entries

More Termcap and Terminfo Syntax

Termcap, Terminfo and the Shell

Writing Termcap and Terminfo Entries

Converting Between Termcap and Terminfo

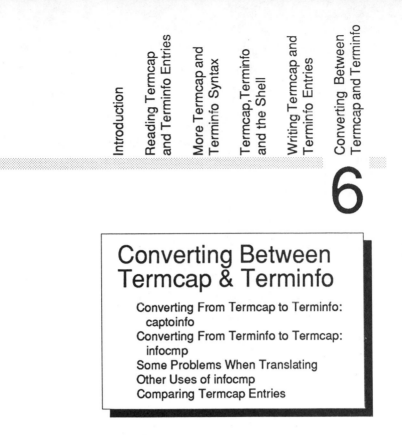

6

Converting Between Termcap & Terminfo

Converting From Termcap to Terminfo: captoinfo

Converting From Terminfo to Termcap: infocmp

Some Problems When Translating

Other Uses of infocmp

Comparing Termcap Entries

This chapter describes how to convert between a *termcap* entry and a *terminfo* entry. It is designed for system administrators or anyone else who might have an interest in converting a file.

For the most part, it is easy to translate between *termcap* and *terminfo*. The *termcap* and *terminfo* databases differ mainly in the names they use for capabilities and in the syntax of the entry: the features described by the capabilities are largely identical. Therefore, the translating programs only have to make the syntactical transformations and vocabulary substitutions. (If only it was so easy with spoken language!)

Converting From Termcap to Terminfo: captoinfo

captoinfo is used to convert a *termcap* file to a *terminfo* file. There are
two different versions of the program that we know of: a public
domain version available on Usenet, and the official version, which is
available with System V Release 3. In our opinion, the public domain
version is less reliable. Since source for the official version is available
at a low cost from the AT&T Toolchest, we recommend that you obtain
and use that version. The effect of the official *captoinfo* is shown in the
example below.

```
$ cat Wyse50.tc
# Wyse50 entry
n9|wy50|Wyse Technology WY-50:\
        :li#24:co#80:am:bs:bw:ul:\
        :cm=\E=%+ %+ :\
        :nd=^L:up=5*^K:do=^J:ho=10^^:bt=EI:\
        :cl=^Z:ce=\ET:cd=EY:\
        :al=\EE:dl=\ER:ic=\EQ:dc=\EW:\
        :so=\EG4:se=\EGO:sg#1:\
        :ue=\EGO:us=\EG8:ug#1\
        :me=\E(EGO:mb=\EG2:mp=\E):mh=\EGp:mr=\EG4:mk=\EG1:\
        :kl=^H:kr=^L:ku=^K:kd=^J:kh=^^:\
        :k1=^A@^M:k2=^AA^M:k3=^AB^M:k4=^AC^M:k5=^AD^M:\
        :k6=^AE^M:k7=^AF^M:k8=^AG^M:k9=^AH^M:k0=^AI^M:
$ captoinfo Wyse50.tc > Wyse50.ti
captoinfo: obsolete 2 character name 'n9' removed.
        synonyms are: 'wy50|Wyse Technology WY-50'
$ cat Wyse50.ti
# Wyse50 entry
wy50|Wyse Technology WY-50,
        bw,     am,     ul,
        cols#80,    lines#24,   xmc#1,
        cbt=\EI,    bel=^G,     cr=\r,
        clear=^Z,   el=\ET,     ed=\EY,
        cup=\E=%p1%' '%+%c%p2%' '%+%c, cud1=\en, home=$<10>^^,
        cub1=\b,    cuf1=\f,    cuu1=$<5*>^K,
        dch1=\EW,   dll=\ER,    blink=\EG2,
        dim=\EGp, prot=\E),   rev=\EG4,
        invis=\EG1,     smso=\EG4, smul=\EG8,
        sgr0=\E(EGO,    rmso=\EGO, rmul=\EGO,
        ich1=\EQ,   ill=\EE,    kbs=\b,
        kcud1=\en, kf0=^AI\r, kf1=^A@\r,
        kf2=^AA\r, kf3=^AB\r, kf4=^AC\r,
        kf5=^AD\r, kf6=^AE\r, kf7=^AF\r,
```

```
kf8=^AG\r, kf9=^AH\r, khome=^^,
kcub1=\b, kcuf1=\f, kcuu1=^K,
nel=\r\en, ind=\en,
```

captoinfo makes all the syntactical and vocabulary substitutions. It also makes some assumptions. It assumes that *bel=^G*, that the *termcap* **nl=** capability is equivalent to both the *terminfo* **cud1=** and **ind=** capabilities, and more. It strips obsolete *termcap* capabilities like **bs**.

The System V Release 3 *captoinfo* strips the first two-character *termcap* name as shown in the example. This makes the *terminfo* names conform to the standard in *term*(5) of the System V manual. The public domain *captoinfo* does not strip the first name. Furthermore, note that the public domain version does not work in the way documented: the public domain *captoinfo* works as a filter and would have appeared in the example as:

```
$ cat Wyse50.tc | captoinfo > Wyse50.ti
```

Converting From Terminfo to Termcap: infocmp

The *infocmp* program is generally used to print out information about compiled *terminfo* entries. However, the *-C* option can be used to convert a compiled *terminfo* entry into the equivalent *termcap* entry.* In the following example, we use *tic*, the *terminfo* compiler, to compile the Wyse-50 *terminfo* source file produced by *captoinfo* in the previous example, and then retrieve it again as a *termcap* entry via *infocmp -C*.

```
$ tic Wyse50.ti
$ infocmp -C wy50 > Wyse50.tc.new
$ cat Wyse50.tc.new
wy50|Wyse Technology WY-50:\
     :li#24:co#80:am:bw:ul:\
     :cm=\E=%+ %+ :\
     :bl=^G:\
```

---

*The *infocmp* program is distributed with System V Release 3 and (like *captoinfo*) is also available from the AT&T Toolchest. See Chapter 2 for more information on the Toolchest.

```
:nd=^L:up=5*^K:do=^J:ho=10^^:bt=\EI:\
:cl=^Z:ce=\ET:cd=\EY:\
:al=\EE:dl=\ER:ic=\EQ:dc=\EW:\
:so=\EG4:se=\EGO:sg#1:\
:ue=\EGO:us=\EG8:\
:me=\E(EGO:mb=\EG2:mp=\E):mh=\EGp:mr=\EG4:mk=\EG1:\
:kl=^H:kr=^L:ku=^K:kd=^J:kh=^^:\
:k1=^A@^M:k2=^AA^M:k3=^AB^M:k4=^AC^M:k5=^AD^M:\
:k6=^AE^M:k7=^AF^M:k8=^AG^M:k9=^AH^M:k0=^AI^M:\
:ko=le,do,nd,up,ho:
```

Note that before we could do anything, we had to compile the *terminfo* source file with *tic*. This is because a *terminfo* source file cannot be accessed by *infocmp*: *infocmp* searches for the terminal keyword (*wy50* in the example) in the */usr/lib/terminfo* hierarchy (or in whatever directory might be specified by the TERMINFO environment variable). Before an entry can be converted to *termcap* form, it has to be compiled and placed into that directory by the *tic* program. Normally, this step would be unnecessary because you would be working from an already compiled *terminfo* entry.

Note that the reconverted *termcap* file is not identical to the original file. The following changes have occurred in the translation:

- The comment line was stripped off, lost when the *terminfo* entry was compiled.

- The first *termcap* name was stripped off by *captoinfo*.

- Some capabilities (such as the *terminfo* *bel=^G* capability) are automatically added by *captoinfo* and will be in the reconverted file.

- Some *termcap* capabilities (such as the *termcap* **bs** capability) do not have an equivalent in *terminfo*, so they were ignored by *captoinfo* and will be missing from the reconverted file.

- Some obsolete capabilities that were not in the *terminfo* entry were assumed by *infocmp*. In the example, note that it added the **ko=** capability, which is obsolete, and in fact was missing from the original *termcap* entry.

- Not all *terminfo* capabilities are translated by *infocmp*: only those capabilities which are currently part of *termcap* are translated. This restriction can be overridden with the *-r* option to *infocmp*, which says to translate all capabilities into *termcap* form.

This emphasizes an important point: when converting between *termcap* and *terminfo*, be ready to do some hand-editing. The main differences will be in the obsolete capabilities and the complicated capabilities. Look especially closely at the string capabilities that take parameters, as errors can occur in the translations. This is one reason why *termcap* users should be familiar with *terminfo* and vice versa.

As with any entry you copy from somewhere else, treat it with skepticism and test it as described in Chapter 5. No matter how close the *terminfo/termcap* translation is, the ancient computer proverb holds: garbage in, garbage out.

Some Problems When Translating

The translating system is not perfect. Consider the following *termcap* example, using the terminal description for the Prime PT100.

In */etc/termcap*, the **k5=** capability reads:

```
:k5=E0%:
```

When we used *captoinfo* to translate it, we got:

```
kf5=E0%,
```

Then we compiled the entire entry with *tic* and tried to translate it back to *termcap* syntax. The **kbs=** capability, however, got garbled as:

```
:.k5=!!! MUST CHANGE BY HAND !!!E0%:
```

What happened? The original *termcap* character contained the character "%". This was transformed into the correct *terminfo* capability by *captoinfo* and compiled without incident. However, when it was decompiled with *infocmp*, *infocmp* thought the "%" character was the start of a parameter encoding sequence. *infocmp* tried to translate that sequence back to *termcap* parameter encoding, found that it was improperly formed, gave up, and printed the warning directly in the capability string. (*infocmp* was considerate enough, however, to comment out the garbled capability with a ".".)

This example demonstrates two points. First, that the argument encoding sequences are the most difficult to translate and the most likely to cause error. Second, that you should look over the result of translation and be ready to edit by hand.

There is one more sidelight to this example. I worked this example on a UNIX System V based computer which uses *terminfo*. */etc/termcap* is mounted on the system but not used. I got the original *termcap* entry from */etc/termcap* and ran *infocmp* to look at the *terminfo* entry that is really used by the system. It gave:

```
kf5=EO%,        (real terminfo entry)
```

not:

```
kf5=E0%,        (terminfo entry translated from termcap)
```

Either the *termcap* or the *terminfo* entry switched the Capital O and the number 0. My guess is that the *termcap* entry is wrong, since the *terminfo* entry is in daily use. The moral of this story is that not all entries are tried and true (not even those distributed by the manufacturer!). Take all *termcap* and *terminfo* entries with a grain of salt.

Other Uses of infocmp

The *infocmp* program is not just for converting from *terminfo* to *termcap* format. As seen in Chapter 2, its default function is to translate a *terminfo* entry from its compiled form into readable output (the *-I* option). The function for which it was developed, however, was to compare two *terminfo* entries, hence the "cmp" part of the name.

Comparing Terminfo Entries with infocmp

If two terminal names are specified, *infocmp* assumes the *-d* option, which says to print a list of capabilities which are different between the two entries.

```
$ infocmp vt100 vt100-w
comparing vt100 to vt100-w
    comparing Booleans.
    comparing numbers.
cols: 80:132.
lines: 24:14.
    comparing strings.
rs2: '\E>\E[?31\E[?41\E[?51\E[?7h\E[?8h','\
    \E>\E[?3h\E[?41\E[?51\E[?8h'.
```

From this comparison, you can see that the only differences between the vt100 and the vt100-w are in the number of columns and lines and in the second reset string.

There are also comparison options to give a listing of the capabilities in common between the two entries (-c), and a list of capabilities missing in both entries (-n). A particularly useful option, however, is the -u option, which says to rephrase the description of the first terminal name as a sum of any other terminal names specified, with *use=* capability strings. For example:

```
$ infocmp -u vt100-w vt100
vt100-w|vt100-w-am|dev vt100 132 cols (w/advanced video),
    cols#132, lines#14,
    rs2='\E>\E[?3h\E[?41\E[?51\E[?8h',
    use=vt100,
```

You can see how powerful a tool *infocmp* can be! *infocmp* can also be used to produce long names for the capabilities (taken from the C variable name listing in **<term.h>**). These names are useful when writing C programs that use terminal capabilities.

```
$ infocmp -L vt100
Terminal type vt100
    vt100|vt100-am|dec vt100 (w/advanced video)
flags
    auto_right_margin, eat_newline_glitch, move_insert_mode,
    move_standout_mode, xon_xoff,

numbers
    columns = 80, init_tabs = 8, lines = 24,
    virtual_terminal = 3,
```

```
strings
     bell = '^G', carriage_return = '\r',
     change_scroll_region = '\E[%i%p1%d;%p2%dr',
     clear_all_tabs = '\E[3g', clear_screen = '\E[H\E[J$<50>',

     ...
```

In addition, there are options to *infocmp* for sorting the fields in a particular order or for printing tracing information as it runs. See the manual page on *infocmp*(1) for more information on all the options provided.

Comparing Termcap Entries

A tool such as *infocmp* suggests the lack of an equivalent for *termcap*. Comparing *termcap* entries can be a bear. As a meager helpmate, we offer the following shell script (which we call *listcap*). This script will extract a single entry from the /etc/termcap file and list its capabilities in a single column in alphabetical order. This will give you a start in comparing two entries.

```
#! /bin/sh
type=${1-$TERM}
echo "Termcap Entry for: $type"
sed -n "/$type|/,/:$/{
     /|/s/^./  &/
     s/:\\\/:/
     s/:/\\
/g
     p
     }
" /etc/termcap | sort -fu
```

This command finds the first entry for a specified terminal type in /etc/termcap. You can supply the name of a terminal type as the first argument on the command line. If you do not, the value of $TERM (your current terminal type) will be used. The alphabetical listing is sent to standard output.

Here is an example of its use:

```
% listcap adm3a
Termcap Entry for: adm3a


        la|adm3a|3a|lsi adm3a
am
bs
cl=1^Z
cm==%+ %+
co#80
do=^J
ho=^^
le=^H
li#24
ma=^K^P
nd=^L
up=^K
```

Part 2: Capability Reference

This part of the book is intended for reference. It describes all of the supported *termcap* and *terminfo* capabilities in detail, organized into functional groups.

There are ten chapters in Part 2:

Chapter 7, *Introduction to the Capabilities*, is crucial to understanding the other nine chapters. It also contains a list of the capabilities covered in the other nine chapters.

Chapter 8, *Screen Dimensions and Cursor Movement*, covers the capabilities necessary to manipulate the screen.

Chapter 9, *Editing the Screen*, discusses those capabilities for adding or deleting text from the terminal screen.

Chapter 10, *Initialization and Reset*, gives a discussion of initialization as handled by both *termcap* and *terminfo*. It also covers tab and margin setting.

Chapter 11, *Special Effects*, covers those features that attract attention on the terminal screen.

Chapter 12, *Special Keys*, lists capabilities that define function keys and other special keys on the keyboard.

Chapter 13, *Padding and XON/XOFF*, describes the mechanisms and syntax involved in padding capabilities and XON/XOFF flow control.

Chapter 14, *Special Terminals*, lists the glitch capabilities necessary for some terminals and also capabilities that are particular to terminals with special enhancements.

Chapter 15, *Equivalent Terminals*, gives a full discussion of the *termcap* **tc=** and the *terminfo* **use=** capabilities and how they are used.

Chapter 16, *Miscellaneous*, lists the odds and ends of capabilities which do not fall into the other groups.

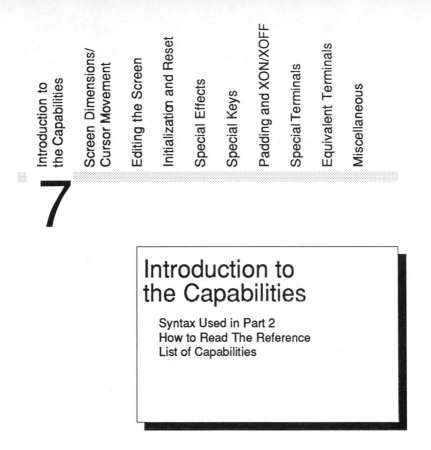

Introduction to
the Capabilities

Introduction to
the Capabilities

Syntax Used in Part 2
How to Read The Reference
List of Capabilities

This and the next nine chapters compose Part 2, the Capability Reference. The capabilities are what *termcap* and *terminfo* are all about. Each capability describes a feature of a terminal, or a function that it can perform. Together, the capabilities compose a complete, detailed description of the terminal's features and idiosyncracies. In Part 1 of this book, we demonstrated how *terminfo* and *termcap* work; in Part 2, we intend to show you what they can actually do.

Each chapter in this reference presents the capabilities in logical groups. Each group is titled and followed by a list of the capabilities covered in that subsection. Before you tackle the rest of Part 2, you should be familiar with the syntax conventions that we use.

Syntax Used in Part 2

The biggest problem in writing this part of the book came about in our decision to cover both *terminfo* and *termcap* together. On one hand, they mirror each other in most functions, so it would be redundant to discuss them separately; on the other hand, we risked confusion and awkward syntax by lumping them together.

Our solution was to list the capabilities together at the beginning of each subsection, to make it clear what topics would be covered and which capabilities were equivalent. Furthermore, we established the convention of writing *terminfo* names in bold italics (for example, *cup=*) and the *termcap* names in bold (for example, **cm=**).

In describing the capabilities themselves, we use the following conventions to distinguish between Boolean, numeric and string capabilities:

* *Boolean capabilities* are written literally, that is, as they would appear in the actual entries.

* *Numeric capabilities* are written with the name of the capability followed by a number sign (#). This is somewhat consistent with the way they would appear in the actual entries; all we omit is the value to be assigned. For example, the capability which describes the number of columns on a terminal screen might appear for an 80-column terminal as *cols#80* in *terminfo*, or **co#80** in *termcap*. We refer to this capability as *cols#* (*terminfo*) and **co#** (*termcap*).

* *String capabilities* are written with the name of the capability followed by a equal sign (=). Like our syntax for numeric capabilities, this is somewhat consistent with strings in the actual entries, since it is only the string to be assigned which is omitted. For example, the capability which describes the string to move backwards one space might appear as *cull=^H* in *terminfo*, or **le=^H** in *termcap*. We refer to this capability as *cull=* (*terminfo*) and **le=** (*termcap*).

Most capabilities are included in all distributions of *termcap* and *terminfo* and are marked in no special way. Your *termcap* system, however, may be less extensive, equal to, or more extensive than BSD 4.3. Furthermore, there are several old *termcap* capabilities that *terminfo* and BSD 4.3 *termcap* do not support and are hence denoted "obsolete," several *terminfo* capabilities that have no equivalent in

BSD 4.3 *termcap*, and many more *terminfo* capabilities that have nominal *termcap* equivalents but are essentially only functional in *terminfo*. Your system documentation is the final arbiter of whether the capability is in your distribution of *termcap*, and your personal experience is the final arbiter of whether it works.

How to Read the Reference

There is a lot of information to be covered in the reference part of this book. The natural questions are how you should approach it and what you should try to learn.

It is important to distinguish between familiarity and detailed knowledge. All users should be acquainted with all capabilities: To use the system effectively, one must know how it works (covered in the previous chapters) and what it does (covered in the following chapters). However, if you are learning about the capabilities for the first time, don't try to memorize all the names and the details! Instead, learn that there are families of capabilities to describe local cursor motion, programming function keys, terminal fonts, and so forth. Become familiar with these families, learn which ones are important and how they interrelate.

Frankly, though, there are times when all you want is to look up the description of a particular capability. Because the *termcap* and *terminfo* names for capabilities are not equivalent, we could not do the obvious and create an alphabetical reference section. Instead, we have tried to organize the capabilities into logical groupings. Then, in Appendix D, we provide a complete alphabetical list of capability names, together with a brief description and a cross reference to the chapter that contains the complete treatment.

If you understand the big picture, it should be fairly easy to find capabilities in the chapters. But if it is not obvious to you from the chapter title or from the table of major headings at the start of each chapter, where the description of a particular capability is to be found, please turn to Appendix D. There is also a complete index at the back of the book.

You will find the details presented in this part of the book be more interesting if you try the capabilities out on your own terminal as described in Chapter 5. For example, when reading about highlighting, look up the standout capabilities in the *termcap* or *terminfo* description for the terminal you are using, and try it out. Detailed knowledge will come when you use the capabilities, whether as a programmer working with them or as a system administrator creating a new database entry.

Introduction to
the Capabilities

Screen Dimensions/
Cursor Movement

Editing the Screen

Initialization and Reset

Special Effects

Special Keys

Padding and XON/XOFF

Special Terminals

Equivalent Terminals

Miscellaneous

8

Screen Dimensions and Cursor Movement

Screen Dimensions
Local Cursor Movement
Parameterized Local Cursor Movement
Absolute Cursor Movement
Scrolling
Miscellaneous Local Movements
Status Lines

Before you can do anything useful on the screen, you need to know how to get the cursor to the proper position. This chapter covers the facilities covered by *termcap* and *terminfo* for manipulating the cursor to reach the desired position. It also covers setting the screen's dimensions, since no screen editor can operate without knowing the dimensions of the screen.

SCREEN
DIMENSIONS

Terminfo	Termcap	Description
lines#	li#	The number of lines on the screen
cols#	co#	The number of columns on the screen

Almost every program that uses the *termcap* or *terminfo* databases needs to know how large the screen is. This information is easily found in the terminal manual; if the terminal manual is missing, you can simply count rows and columns on a screenful of characters to determine your terminal's dimensions.

- *Lines on the Screen:*
  The number of lines on the screen is represented by the *lines#* capability in *terminfo* and by the li# capability in *termcap*. If your terminal has a status line as well, you should refer to the discussion on status lines at the end of this chapter.

- *Columns on the Screen:*
  The number of columns on the screen is represented by the *cols#* capability in *terminfo* and by the co# capability in *termcap*.

In a *terminfo* system, the values for *lines#* and *cols#* can be overridden by the $LINES and $COLUMNS environment variables. Thus, a terminal which can change its dimensions on the setup menu does not need two almost identical *terminfo* entries to toggle between but can simply redefine $LINES or $COLUMNS as needed.

LOCAL
CURSOR MOVEMENT

Terminfo	Termcap	Description
cuu1=	**up=**	Move cursor up.
cud1=	**do=**	Move cursor down.
cub1=	**le=**	Move cursor left.
cuf1=	**nd=**	Non-destructive space (cursor moves to right).
home=	**ho=**	Move cursor home (upper lefthand corner).
ll=	**ll=**	Move cursor to lower left corner.
cr=	**cr=**	Carriage return character (usually ^M).

These capabilities are pretty much self-explanatory. However, there are some special cases which require some discussion here.

- *Moving Up and Down:*
  Moving up from the top line (with **up=** in *termcap* and *cuu1=* in *terminfo*) and down from the bottom line (with **do=** in *termcap* and *cud1=* in *terminfo*) have undefined effects. They work logically for some terminals and not for others, so programs should avoid these cases.

- *Moving to the Left:*
  Movement one space to the left is described by the **le=** capability in *termcap* and the *cub1=* capability in *terminfo*. If the cursor is in the first column, this capability has an undefined effect unless **bw** (backwards wrap) is specified, in which case moving left from the first column moves the cursor to the last column of the previous line. This makes things easier for the system administrator who is writing the capability and tells programmers to avoid this case. See Chapter 16 for more information on the backwards wrap capability.

- *Moving to the Right:*
Movement one space to the right is determined by the **nd=** capability in *termcap* and the *cuf1=* capability in *terminfo*. The effect of issuing this effect from the last column is never defined, not even when **am** (automargin) is specified. See Chapter 16 for more information on the **am** capability.

- *Home and Lower Left:*
The Home and lower left capabilities respectively describe movement of the cursor to the upper left and the lower left of the screen for multi-page terminals. Note that this movement is relative to the screen, not to the display memory. The Home capability is described by *home=* in *terminfo* and **ho=** in *termcap*. The lower left capability is called **ll=** in both *termcap* and *terminfo*.

- *Carriage Return:*
termcap assumes that the carriage return character is ^M, so *termcap* entries need to specify **cr=** only for terminals with a different carriage return character. On *terminfo* systems, *cr=* should always be specified, since it does not assume ^M.

The **cr=** capability may require padding on some terminals. Although *termcap* entries only require **cr=** for a non-standard carriage return, you may want to include it anyhow to specify padding in the capability.

For most every terminal, the sequence for moving up, down, left, or right one space is a simple control character. If you have arrow keys on your keyboard, the sequence sent by the arrow keys often coincides with the the sequence needed to move in that direction. For example, if your up-arrow key (↑) issues the sequence "ESC-[A", then often the move-up sequence will be the same, so both the **ku=** (*termcap*) or *kcuu1=* (*terminfo*) capability and the **up=** (*termcap*) or *cuu1=* (*terminfo*) capability will be defined as "\E[A". See Chapter 12 for more information on arrow keys and key capability twins.

Methods for finding out what sequence is sent by a key are described in Chapter 5.

On terminals that do not have a true lower left capability, one can often be built from capabilities that the terminal does have. For terminals that wrap from the top of the screen to the bottom, the lower left capability can be constructed by issuing the commands to move the cursor home and then up one line. For example, if your terminal moves to HOME with ^A, and up one line with ^B, it might move to the lower left with the sequence ^A^B. (This will not work for all terminals.)

PARAMETERIZED
LOCAL CURSOR MOVEMENT

Terminfo	Termcap	Description
cuu=	UP=	Move cursor up a number of rows.
cud=	DO=	Move cursor down a number of rows.
cub=	LE=	Move cursor left a number of columns.
cuf=	RI=	Move cursor right a number of columns.

The four parameterized local movement capabilities differ from their non-parameterized siblings described previously in that they each take a single run time parameter that tells how far to move the cursor in the given direction. Like the local cursor movement commands described above, they move the cursor relative to its initial position. Each may require some padding in your terminal entry.

Not all terminals have these capabilities. They can be used by programs to improve efficiency, but even if available, they can be omitted from a terminal description. Programmers should not use any of these capabilities to move over the edge of the screen (top, bottom, left or right), as the effect is undefined.

See Chapter 3 for more information about parameters and how to encode them.

ABSOLUTE
CURSOR MOVEMENT

Terminfo	Termcap	Description
cup=	cm=	Move cursor to row #1 and column #2 (absolutely essential).
mrcup=	CM=	Move cursor to row #1 and column #2 relative to memory.
hpa=	ch=	Move cursor horizontally on its line to column #1.
vpa=	cv=	Move cursor vertically in its column to line #1.
sc=	sc=	Save absolute cursor position.
rc=	rc=	Restore cursor to position saved by sc=

For moving the cursor to a specified coordinate on the screen, there are four capabilities available: one for absolute cursor movement, one for cursor movement relative to data stored in terminal memory, one for only horizontal movement, and one for only vertical movement. In addition, there are save and restore capabilities which allow specific cursor positions to be returned to later. All of these capabilities may require padding in your terminal entry.

- *Absolute Cursor Movement:*
  The absolute cursor movement capability must be written and debugged for all efficient terminals. It describes how to move the cursor to any spot on the screen. This capability is described by cm= in *termcap* and *cup=* in *terminfo*. While it is one of the most difficult capabilities to write, absolute cursor movement is essential to many programs. All terminals support absolute cursor motion, so programs depend on it to be properly described in the terminal's *termcap* or *terminfo* definition.

  In writing a *termcap* or *terminfo* entry, the absolute cursor motion capability needs to have two arguments specified: the row address and the column address, encoded into the command string issued to the terminal. Thus, the definition string is part command characters (which are output just as they are, starting from the left) and part encoded arguments. Both *termcap* and *terminfo* use percent signs (%) to indicate argument encoding instructions, but they use the "%" escapes differently. See Chapter 3 for more information on encoding arguments in *termcap* and *terminfo*.

- *Memory Relative Addressing:*
  A few terminals use memory relative cursor addressing instead of (or in addition to) screen relative cursor addressing—that is, they have several pages of memory, and the screen shows only a subset of the memory at a time. The capability for computing rows and columns relative to the base of that memory is called **CM=** in *termcap* and **mrcup=** in *terminfo*.

- *Vertical and Horizontal Motion:*
  The vertical and horizontal capabilities are one-dimensional cousins of the absolute motion capability. They are limited to movement in one dimension, keeping the other dimension fixed. These capabilities are called **vpa=** and **hpa=** in *terminfo*, and **cv=** and **ch=** in *termcap*.

  Do not include these capabilities in your database entry if they are slower than absolute motion on your terminal (unless padding information is included), since they are useful to programs only when they are faster than the two-dimensional capability moving in one dimension. Unlike the absolute motion capability, programs do not depend on the existence of vertical and horizontal capabilities.

- *Save and Restore:*
  The save and restore capabilities (**sc=** and **rc=** in both *terminfo* and *termcap*) provide one last way to perform absolute cursor movement. On the few terminals that support these capabilities, **sc=** should be assigned the string for saving the current cursor position. Once it is used, the cursor can then be moved arbitrarily. The string to return to the saved position should be described in the **rc=** capability. Only one position can be saved at a time.

  The save cursor and restore cursor strings can be incorporated into other capabilities for terminals which perform most of a function, but end up leaving the cursor in the wrong place. For example, some terminals have imperfect "to status line" and "from status line" capabilities, which should leave the cursor where it started.

Incorporating the save and restore cursor capabilities into those capabilities can fix that problem. See the section later in this chapter for more information on status lines.

sc= and rc= are relatively new capabilities in *termcap*, and while useful, most programs do not depend on them. They are almost essential, however, if scrolling regions are specified (cs= in *termcap* or *csr=* in *terminfo*). Terminals which define scrolling regions almost always have sc= and rc= capabilities. There are many programs which, when using scrolling regions, depend on sc= and rc= to be there. See the following section for more information on scrolling regions.

SCROLLING

Terminfo	Termcap	Description
ind=	sf=	Scroll forward one line.
ri=	sr=	Scroll reverse (backwards) one line.
indn=	SF=	Scroll forward #1 lines.
rin=	SR=	Scroll reverse (backwards) #1 lines.
csr=	cs=	Change scrolling region of screen to rows #1 to #2.
da	da	Display retained above screen (usually multi-page terminals).
db	db	Display retained below screen (usually multi-page terminals).

All the string capabilities described here may need padding.

- *Scrolling Forwards and Backwards:*
  Enter the string for a forward scroll into the **sf=** capability in *termcap*, or the **ind=** capability in *terminfo*. A forward scroll is one which shifts the display up one line: The top line is deleted, and a blank line is added at the bottom. When scrolling, the cursor should stay on the same row and column position. This scroll is not performed by the software (by redrawing the screen character by character as the text is shifted up one line) but by the terminal hardware.

A reverse scroll shifts the screen down by deleting the bottom line and adding a blank line at the top. It can be simulated by adding a blank line at the top of the screen. The reverse scroll capability is called **sr=** in *termcap* and **ri=** in *terminfo*.

Some systems are more restrictive and demand that forward scrolling be done with the cursor at the first character of the last line, and backward scrolling with the cursor at the first character of the top line. This allows a forward scroll to be simulated with a carriage return.

• *Parameterized Scrolling:*
The parameterized scrolling variations each take a single run time parameter, which tells how many lines to scroll. In *termcap*, these capabilities are **SF=** (to scroll forwards) and **SR=** (to scroll backwards). In *terminfo*, these capabilities are called *indn=* and *rin=*.

Some terminals will not support the parameterized scrolling capabilities, so programs should be prepared to scroll one line at a time if need be. See Chapter 3 for full information about run time parameters.

• *Changing the Scrolling Region:*
Some terminals (notably the DEC vt100) can scroll a part of their screen while leaving other lines above and below the region untouched. If your terminal can do this, define the string to change the scrolling region in the **cs=** capability in *termcap*, or the *csr=* capability in *terminfo*. A scroll applied to a region has the usual effect: it deletes the top line, shifts, and adds a line at the bottom. When finished with the new scrolling region, a program should use this same capability to restore the scrolling region size to the whole screen.

The new scrolling region is specified by two run time parameters, the first specifying the number of the top line and the second specifying the number of the bottom line, given that the top line of the screen is line 0. See Chapter 3 for more information about encoding arguments.

If a terminal definition contains the scrolling region capability, the **sc=** and **rc=** capabilities (save cursor and restore cursor) must also be specified. Many programs which use scrolling regions depend on the **sc=** and **rc=** capabilities.

There are some rare terminals with non-destructive scrolling regions. If you have one of these terminals, we recommend that the capability be omitted from the terminal entry. Otherwise, an unsuspecting program may produce garbled output.

Two warnings for programmers: The cursor position is undefined after changing the scrolling region, so after using this capability the cursor should be moved into the scrolling region with **cm=** (*termcap*) or *cup=* (*terminfo*). The cursor should not be moved out of the scrolling region until you are finished with the region.

- *Scrolling on Multi-page Terminals:*
  On a multi-page terminal, adding a line of scrolling may push a line onto another page, and scrolling in the opposite direction brings that line back. Similarly, deleting a line can also bring a line in from off the screen. Programs that use scrolling need to know this to adjust their behavior, and for that reason, you should specify the Boolean **da** and **db** capabilities for multi-page terminals (both *termcap* and *terminfo*).

  For example, *vi* assumes that lines scrolled in will always be blank. If the **da** and **db** capabilities are set, *vi* clears the line before it scrolls it off the screen so that the line will be empty if it is scrolled back. If the terminal is using redefinable scrolling regions as described directly above, then the lines are lost regardless of **da** and **db**.

MISCELLANEOUS LOCAL MOVEMENTS

Terminfo	Termcap	Description
nel=	**nw=**	Newline command (carriage return, then down).
	bs	Terminal uses ^H to backspace (obsolete).
hu=	**hu=**	Halfline up: move cursor up half a linefeed.
hd=	**hd=**	Halfline down: move cursor down half a linefeed.

- *Newlines:*
  The newline capability describes how to move the cursor to the first column of the next line. The command may or may not clear the remainder of the line that the cursor was on. The newline capability is described by **nw=** in *termcap* and by *nel=* in *terminfo* (BSD 4.3 only). Proportional padding may be needed.

  termcap also has a **nl=** capability for terminals which do not use the standard ^J. The **nl=** capability is obsolete and has no match in *terminfo*. It is discussed more fully in Chapter 12.

- *Backspace Capability:*
  The **bs** capability, which was an important capability in older *termcap*, is obsolete in *terminfo* and BSD 4.3. On older systems, the Boolean capability **bs** is specified for terminals which use ^H as the backspace character. For terminals which use something other than ^H to backspace, the **bc=** capability must be used (which is also obsolete in *terminfo*). See Chapter 12 for more information on **bc=**.

  In *terminfo*, there are no capabilities analogous to **bs** or **bc=**. Instead, the backspace character should be specified in the *cub1=* *terminfo* capability. See the section in this chapter entitled ''Local Cursor Movement'' for more information on *cub1=*.

- *Halfline Capabilities:*

  The halfline capabilities are defined on only a handful of terminals. They move the cursor half a line up or down respectively, usually for creating a subscript or a superscript. This is more common on hardcopy terminals (which actually move the paper) than on video terminals, so these capabilities are predominantly for hardcopy terminals. For display terminals, programs should not move off the screen with halflines, as the effect is undefined. In both *termcap* and *terminfo*, halflines are described by **hu=** and **hd=**; however, when you are writing a new terminal description, you can usually omit these capabilities.

  See Chapter 14 for more information on hardcopy terminals.

For terminals that do not have a proper newline character, it is sometimes possible to construct the newline from a carriage return and a line feed. The newline capability is useful for terminals with limited absolute motion capabilities.

Clever programs can survive with limited cursor motion capabilities. For example, if your terminal has dimensions of the screen and the clear capability defined, it can run *vi* with only **cr=** and ***cuu1=*** (or **up=** in *termcap*), because it can use the newline character to go down, it can retype the character the cursor is on to go right, and it can type a carriage return, and then retype the line to the character before the cursor to go left. Home and lower left are not essential, as they can be substituted for by multiple ups or downs, or by direct cursor movement. Of course, it is much more efficient to have the full set of cursor motion commands available.

STATUS LINES

Terminfo	Termcap	Description
hs	**hs**	Terminal has status line.
tsl=	**ts=**	To Status: send cursor to #1 column of status line.
fsl=	**fs=**	From Status: return cursor to its position before going to status line.
dsl=	**ds=**	Disable Status: turn off or erase the status line.
eslok	**es**	Escape sequences and special characters work in status line.
wsl#	**ws#**	Specify width of status line if different from rest of screen.

Some terminals have an extra "status line" at the bottom of the screen. A status line is outside the lines normally used by the software. Ordinary terminal output should not affect the status line, only the special status commands described here.

There are two ways that terminals provide status lines. Some terminals, such as the Heathkit h19, truly have an extra line: the h19 has 25 lines, 24 for text and the twenty-fifth being the status line. Other terminals, such as the DEC vt100, can emulate a status line by changing the scrolling region to scroll all but the last line (with the **cs=** capability in *termcap*, or the *csr=* capability in *terminfo*). This leaves the last line free to be used as a status line.

The **hs** capability (both *termcap* and *terminfo*) should be specified for terminals that have a status line of either sort.

If the status line is created by changing the scrolling region, then the command to change the scrolling region should be put in the initialization string for the terminal. To be absolutely safe, you could omit changing the scrolling region in that database entry, so that the user could not reset the scrolling region to the full window size and thus destroy the status line. Thus, you could have two database entries for such a terminal, one without a status line and with a change scrolling region, and one with a status line and without a change scrolling region. Unfortunately, there is not yet a string capability to specifically turn on the status line, while there is one (**ds=** in *termcap* and *dsl=* in *terminfo*) to turn it off.

- *Moving the Cursor to and from the Status Line:*
  To move to and from the status line, there are two parameterized capabilities. The **ts=** capability in *termcap* and the *tsl=* capability in *terminfo* moves the cursor to the column of the status line specified by the single parameter. To return the cursor to the position it was at before entering the status line, use the **fs=** capability in *termcap*, or the *fsl=* capability in *terminfo*. If the terminal does not return the cursor to its old cursor position, you can do so manually by coding the save cursor and restore cursor commands into these capabilities, discussed earlier in this chapter. See Chapter 3 for more information on specifying parameters.

- *Disabling the Status Line:*
  The **ds=** capability in *termcap* (or the *dsl=* capability in *terminfo*) specifies a command which disables the status line. On some systems, it can also be used for commands which clear the status line. A simple clear of the status line can sometimes be simulated by moving the cursor to the status line, issuing the delete line command, and then restoring the cursor to its original position.

- *Escape Sequences in the Status Line:*
  Specify the Boolean capability **es** in *termcap*, or *eslok* in *terminfo*, if escape sequences and special characters (such as tabs) work correctly in the status line.

- *Resizing the Status Line:*
  The status line is assumed to be the same width as the rest of the screen, unless the **ws#** capability (in *termcap*) or the *wsl=* capability (in *terminfo*) is used to specify a different width.

Introduction to
the Capabilities

Screen Dimensions/
Cursor Movement

Editing the Screen

Initialization and Reset

Special Effects

Special Keys

Padding and XON/XOFF

Special Terminals

Equivalent Terminals

Miscellaneous

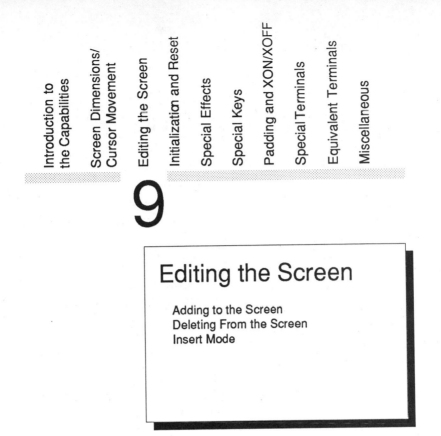

9

Editing the Screen

Adding to the Screen
Deleting From the Screen
Insert Mode

This chapter discusses the capabilities that describe how to insert and delete text on the screen. It covers not only the capabilities for inserting or deleting characters and lines, but also for entering and leaving insert mode and delete mode.

ADDING
TO THE SCREEN

Terminfo	Termcap	Description
ill=	al=	Add line below line with cursor.
il=	AL=	Add #1 lines above below line with cursor.
rep=	rp=	Repeat character #1 #2 times (predominantly *terminfo*)

There are two capabilities to add new blank lines to the screen, and one to add a specified character to the screen a specified number of times. All three require proportional padding in your terminal entry.

- *Adding a Single Line:*
  The string to add a line below the present line should be defined in the **al=** capability in *termcap*, or the *ill=* capability in *terminfo*. Since some terminals do not add a line correctly if the cursor is in the middle of a line, the convention is that programs should only use this capability when the terminal is in the first column of the line. When this capability is used, it should leave the cursor at the start of the new, blank line.

  The *vi* editor expects your terminal to have this capability and can use it to simulate a reverse scroll by going to the top of the screen, adding a blank line, and then filling it with the text it should contain.

  When this capability is used, the bottom line is pushed off the bottom of the screen and is usually lost forever. On some terminals (mostly multi-page terminals), these lines can be saved in memory, in which case you should refer to the discussion of the **db=** capability in Chapter 8.

- *Adding a Number of Lines:*
  Specify the string to add several lines at once in the *il=* capability in *terminfo*, and in the **AL=** capability in *termcap*. These capabilities take a single run time parameter, specifying how many lines to add.

Like *il1=* and *al=*, they should be used only when the cursor is in the first column.

Setting the scroll region or setting a window affects which line is pushed off the screen when lines are added (and where lines are pulled from when lines are deleted). See Chapter 8 for more information on scrolling.

- *The Repeat Capability:*
Put the string for sending a specified character a specified number of times in the *rep=* capability in *terminfo*, or the the *rp=* capability in *termcap*. It should leave the cursor at the end of the new characters. It takes two parameters: the character to be sent and the number of times to send it. This capability is primarily a *terminfo* capability, so although it is defined in BSD 4.3 *termcap*, few *termcap* systems use it. Programmers should not depend on it, and writers of *termcap* entries should give it a low priority. Repeating characters is for efficiency only, is not possible on many terminals and is not implemented on many *termcap* systems.

The repeat capability may need padding proportional to the number of characters that are output. *termcap* and *terminfo* have no direct way to do this, since they either output a fixed amount of padding or output padding proportional to the number of lines affected. On *terminfo* systems, however, a way to do this is to use the second argument (the number of times the character is to be repeated) to output an appropriate integer as part of the pad specification. This integer will be used by *tputs* as the integer representing padding. An example of this is shown below, assuming that the terminal needs 5 milliseconds of padding for each character sent.

```
rep=...$<%p2%{5}%*%d>
```

(where " ... " represents the command part of the *rep=* capability). On *termcap* systems, an equivalent method is not possible due to the limitations of the *termcap* parameter encoding sequences. See Chapter 3 for more information on the syntax for encoding parameters in both *termcap* and *terminfo*.

This generally works with all capabilities that have arguments. It does require that the arguments be processed before the padding is processed, which the *terminfo* routines do specify.

DELETING
FROM THE SCREEN

Terminfo	Termcap	Description
clear=	**cl=**	Clear screen. Cursor to upper left.
ed=	**cd=**	Clear display after cursor.
el=	**ce=**	Clear to end of line.
ell=	**cb=**	Clear from beginning of line to cursor (not in BSD 4.3).
dll=	**dl=**	Delete line that cursor is on.
dl=	**DL=**	Delete #1 lines including and below line with cursor.
dch1=	**dc=**	Delete character at cursor. Must be defined if delete mode defined.
dch=	**DC=**	Delete #1 characters starting at cursor.
smdc=	**dm=**	Begin delete mode.
rmdc=	**ed=**	End delete mode.
ech=	**ec=**	"Erase" #1 characters starting at cursor.

There are eight capabilities that delete text from the screen.

* *Clearing Text:*
  The clear screen capability (described by **cl=** in *termcap* and *clear=* in *terminfo*) is essential to many programs. If your terminal does not have a true hardware clear, you can create a clear command by writing your capability as a sequence of enough newlines to clear the screen, and appending the Home command sequence so that the cursor ends up in the upper left corner.

  The clear display capability (**cd=** in *termcap* and *ed=* in *terminfo*) is for clearing the display below the cursor but leaving the text above intact. Some terminals require that the clear display after cursor capability be issued only when the cursor is at the first column of the line, in which case it clears the entire line. Proportional padding may be necessary for both the clear screen and the clear display after cursor capabilities.

The string to clear from the cursor to the end of the line should be specified in the *el=* capability in *terminfo*, and in the ce= capability in *termcap*. The capability for clearing from the beginning of the line to the cursor (cb= in *termcap* and *ell=* in *terminfo*) is not defined in BSD 4.3 and is not available on most *termcap* systems. Some padding may be necessary for clearing part of a line.

- *Deleting Lines:*
  The string for deleting a single line should be specified in *dll=* in *terminfo*, and in dl= in *termcap*. The parameterized string for deleting more than one line should be placed in *dl=* in *terminfo* and in **DL=** in *termcap*. Proportional padding may be necessary.

The line deletion capabilities actually delete lines in their entirety, with the lines below moving up to fill the gap that is left. New blank lines are usually added at the bottom of the screen, but on some terminals (especially multi-page terminals), deleting a line will bring back a line of text that was earlier pushed off the bottom of the screen. Specify **db** for such terminals, discussed in Chapter 8.

Do not define dl= if the terminal does not move up the lines below, as *vi* will think you have the true dl= capability and so will not work around the limitation. Setting the scroll region or setting a window affects where lines are pulled back on by dl= (as well as which line is pushed off the screen when lines are added).

Some terminals may require that dl= and DL= only be used from the first column of the screen.

- *Deleting Characters:*
  Two capabilities are available to delete characters on a line but leave the rest of the line intact. The string to delete a single character should be specified in the *dch1=* capability in *terminfo* and in the **dc=** capability in *termcap*. The parameterized capability for character deletion is *dch=* in *terminfo* and DC= in *termcap*. Your terminal may need to be in a special mode to execute the delete character capabilities.

Proportional padding may be necessary.

- *Entering and Leaving Delete Mode:*
  To delete the character under the cursor, some terminals need to enter a specific delete mode, issue the delete character command, then leave delete mode. These terminals thus require all three capabilities: begin delete mode, delete character, and end delete mode. Many terminals do not need to enter delete mode; to maintain consistency with insert mode, however, blank delete mode and end delete mode capabilities are often included in entries.

  On some terminals, delete mode and insert mode are identical. Programs that check for this can improve their efficiency when inserting and deleting consecutively by avoiding the commands to switch between modes.

  If the strings to begin and end delete mode are defined, you must also define **dc=** (*termcap*) or *dch1=* (*terminfo*). See the section on deleting from the screen (earlier in this chapter) for more information on **dc=** and *dch1=*.

  Note that delete mode never applies to the delete line or clear capabilities. If at all, it applies only to the delete character capabilities.

- *The Erase Capability:*
  The parameterized erase capability replaces the specified number of characters (starting at the cursor) with blanks. The cursor position should be unchanged. Programs should be sure that the parameter does not extend past the right margin, as the effect of such commands is undefined. The string for erasing characters should be specified in the **ech=** capability in *terminfo*, and in the **ec=** capability in *termcap*. Proportional padding may be necessary.

Where the Cursor Ends Up

There are two parts to each of the deletion commands: they must delete text as directed, and then put the cursor in a correct position. If your terminal correctly deletes text but does not leave the cursor where programs will expect it, you will have to be creative. See if you can get the desired effect by combining the terminal's delete command with a cursor movement command.

For example, the clear screen capability should leave the cursor at the home position at the top left of the (now empty) screen. If your terminal uses ^A as a clear sequence that clears the screen but leaves the cursor where it was, and also provides ^B as a home sequence, make your clear capability be cl=^A^B. The other clear capabilities, and the delete character capability, should all leave the cursor where it was. The delete line capability should leave the cursor at the start of the deleted line.

INSERT
MODE

Terminfo	Termcap	Description
smir=	im=	Begin insert mode.
rmir=	ei=	End insert mode.
ich1=	ic=	Insert character: open a space so that the next character after this string can be inserted.
ich=	IC=	Parameterized character insert: open up #1 spaces for characters to be inserted into.
in	in	Terminal inserts nulls, not spaces, to fill whitespace in screen.
ip=	ip=	Insert pad: pad time and any special chars needed after inserting a char in insert mode.
mir	mi	Terminal cursor movement commands work while in insert mode.

Many terminals do not just have an add line command; they have a complete insert mode. In insert mode, characters can be inserted in the middle of a line, with all the characters that follow being shifted to the right to make space. If your terminal does not have an insert mode capability, *vi* inserts characters by initially overwriting the old text, then restoring it after the insertion when you are through entering new text.

- *Entering and Leaving Insert Mode:*
  Define **im=** and **ei=** in *termcap*, or *smir=* and *rmir=* in *terminfo*, as the strings to enter and leave insert mode. Older *termcap*-based versions of *vi* require that you specify these capabilities if you have an insert mode, even if your terminal does not require any special command to get into insert mode. Humor *vi* for such terminals by defining a null insert mode capability. (Newer programs should not have this requirement.)

On some old, generally obsolete terminals, the strings to enter and leave insert mode are identical, so programs must keep track of whether or not the terminal is in insert mode.

On some terminals, the commands to enter delete mode and to enter insert mode are identical, meaning that delete mode and insert mode are identical. Programs that check for this can improve their efficiency when inserting and deleting consecutively by avoiding the commands to switch between modes.

- *Insert Mode Command String:*
  Some terminals require that a command string be sent with each character to be inserted, even though they are in insert mode. This command string is usually used to open up a space in the line for the character to be inserted into. Specify this string with **ic=** in *termcap* and *ich1=* in *terminfo*. As with the previously discussed capabilities, older *termcap*-based versions of *vi* require that these capabilities be defined on every terminal that has insert mode. If your terminal requires no special insert character sequence while in insert mode, humor *vi* by defining a null insert character capability.

  For insertion of several characters, there is a parameterized insert character capability, called **IC=** in *termcap* and *ich=* in *terminfo*. It prepares the terminal so that the specified number of characters to follow will be inserted before the cursor. Usually, the preparation consists of opening up the necessary number of spaces, and the cursor is left where it started. This capability is not required by *vi*.

  By the BSD 4.3 *termcap* and *terminfo* definition, programs should be in insert mode before using this capability, although in practice most terminals do not require it.

- *Nulls or Blanks?*
  Some terminals send nulls rather than spaces when they have to create white space on the screen. Both show up on the screen as blanks, but the terminal will delete the nulls when you insert characters on top of them, while it will shift blanks to the right. Few terminals insert nulls, but those that do should have the Boolean **in** capability specified (both *termcap* and *terminfo*), which tells programs that the terminal distinguishes between spaces (sent by hitting the space bar) and nulls (the character sent by \200) when it is displaying the screen.

To find out whether your terminal inserts nulls, perform the following test (invented by Bill Joy):

> Clear the screen, put your terminal in local mode, and type "abc→def" (where the "→" represents the right arrow key). Your terminal will display "abc   def." Use the left arrow key to move back to the start of the blank space and place the terminal in insert mode. Now type "123". If your screen looks like "abc123def," your terminal sent nulls that it then wrote over, and you should include the **in** capability. If your screen shows "abc123   def," your terminal sent blanks when you used the left arrow key, and **in** should not be specified.

- *Insert Padding:*
  A pad, as described in Chapter 3, is a length of time that the computer should wait after sending a specific command sequence. It is measured in milliseconds and can be made proportional to the number of lines affected. The amount of padding you should allow when you insert a character should be placed in the **ip=** capability in both *termcap* and *terminfo*. This capability seems somewhat redundant, but it is also used as padding when entering or leaving insert mode, and those capabilities do not allow for padding to be defined within them.

  Two examples of the **ip=** format are **ip=16** or **ip=17*** for a 16- and a proportional 17-millisecond delay, respectively. In addition, **ip=** allows you to specify any magic characters or strings that should be sent after inserting a character in insert mode.

  Few terminals need the **ip=** capability.

  There is also a padding capability analogous to **ip=**, but which pads after every character typed (regardless of insert mode). This capability is called *rmp=* in *terminfo*, and **rP=** in *termcap* (except for BSD 4.3). This capability is more fully discussed in Chapter 13.

- *Moving in Insert Mode:*
  Some terminals can make absolute screen movements while in insert mode and still be in insert mode after the cursor movement command. If your terminal can do this, specify the Boolean **mi** capability in *termcap*, or the *mir* capability in *terminfo*. Your terminal manual may tell you if movement in insert mode is not possible; however, do not take lack of a warning as proof of its safety. It is best to test it out on your own terminal.

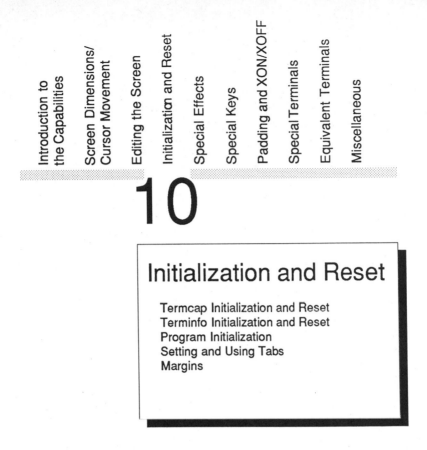

Introduction to
the Capabilities

Screen Dimensions/
Cursor Movement

Editing the Screen

Initialization and Reset

Special Effects

Special Keys

Padding and XON/XOFF

Special Terminals

Equivalent Terminals

Miscellaneous

10

Initialization and Reset

Termcap Initialization and Reset
Terminfo Initialization and Reset
Program Initialization
Setting and Using Tabs
Margins

This chapter discusses not only the initialization and reset capabilities but also those for setting tabs and margins.

For initialization and reset, we will discuss *termcap* and *terminfo* separately, since they use use distinct (but related) initialization and reset capabilities. Actually, the *terminfo* initialization and reset system is really a superset of the *termcap* system, but while BSD 4.3 *termcap* defines capabilities equivalent to the *terminfo* capabilities, it does not use them. To minimize confusion, the two sets of capabilities are covered in two separate (and equal) sections.

termcap users should read the following section and only refer to the *terminfo* section if they want to learn the equivalent capability names. *terminfo* users should read the *terminfo* section and refer back to the following section as needed. Some advanced *termcap* systems (beyond

BSD 4.3) may have the *terminfo* superset of initialization capabilities; users of those systems should follow the *terminfo* initialization instructions.

All *curses* programs assume that the terminal has been initialized with the initialization sequences described here; this initialization only needs to be done once during a login session. For this reason, the initialization is usually done within *profile* (for Bourne shell users) or *.login* (for C shell users). In System V, the initialization is done by *tputinit*. See Chapter 4 for more information on *tput*. In BSD, the initialization is done by *tset*.

TERMCAP
INITIALIZATION AND RESET

Termcap	*Description*
is=	Initialization string for terminal initialization.
if=	Initialization file containing long initialization strings.
rs=	Reset string: reset terminal to sane modes.
rf=	Reset file containing long reset strings.

The initialization capabilities contain sequences of commands that should be issued during login. The commands will have their desired effect on the terminal: setting or clearing tabs, arranging a special mode, switching the style of the cursor, clearing the screen—whatever commands are written into the initialization sequence. See Chapter 4 for more information on *tset* and terminal initialization.

The key question is when the different initialization capabilities are to be used. The answer to that question allows you to decide what features you want to put in the various initialization commands.

* *The Initialization Strings:*
  In *termcap*, **is=** is the basic terminal initialization sequence, which will be used by *tset* when you log in to set features you will always want your terminal to have.

  Many terminals also allow initialization features to be set by switches on the terminal. Some terminals have a software reset command; it is sometimes appropriate for initialization, sometimes too powerful and may be more appropriate for the **rs=** reset string. The system administrator must decide which features to set on all terminals with *termcap* and which to leave to the switches on the individual terminal.

  Tab stops should be placed on every eighth character. Setting tabs usually require a long string of special, terminal-dependent commands.

- *Initialization Files:*
  If the initialization command sequence is too long (i.e., greater than 80 characters), you may place it in a file and enter the absolute pathname to that file in the **if=** capability. This usually occurs when there are long tab setting sequences, so such files often reside in the */usr/lib/tabset* directory.

  It is up to you to decide whether the initialization string should go in **if=** or **is=**. The initialization file capability is rarely needed; there are only eight files in */usr/lib/tabset* on our System V based machine. If both **is=** and **if=** are set, the **is=** command string is issued first.

- *Terminal Reset:*
  The reset capabilities are relatively new features that are absent from many older systems. Older programs may use the initialization commands to simulate a reset. The **rs=** capability is analogous to **is=**, and the **rf=** capability is analogous to **if=**. They should be able to reset the terminal from a totally unknown state.

  The reset capabilities usually contain the initialization commands, plus commands that would be unnecessary and annoying when logging in (such as setting the DEC vt100 to 80 columns) but are needed to get you out of a jam. If the terminal has a software reset button, it may be appropriate for **rs=**. If the terminal has a RESET button or key, the characters that it sends might be all you need. The **rs=** and **rf=** capabilities are used by the *reset* program in that order.

124

TERMINFO
INITIALIZATION AND RESET

Terminfo	Termcap	Description
iprog=	iP=	Init program: initialize terminal at login.
is1=	i1=	Init string 1: initialize terminal at login.
is2=	is=	Init string 2: initialize terminal at login.
is3=	i3=	Init string 3: initialize terminal at login.
if=	if=	Initialization file for long initialization commands at login.
rs1=	r1=	Reset string 1: reset terminal to sane modes.
rs2=	r2=	Reset string 2: reset terminal to sane modes.
rs3=	r3=	Reset string 3: reset terminal to sane modes.
rf=	rf=	Reset file: name of file containing reset codes.

The *terminfo* initialization commands serve the same purposes as the *termcap* commands: initialization for login, and reset to restore sanity. They differ in complexity.

- *The Initialization Capabilities:*
  There are three initialization capabilities to make it easy to customize initialization for similar terminals. They are *is1=*, *is2=*, and *is3=*. You can put the common initialization commands in one string for all the similar terminals and the terminal specific commands in the other two strings. By convention, most initialization is done by *is2=* (and so is compatible with converted *termcap* entries written with only *is=*.) *is1=* and *is3=* are used only for special cases.

If the initialization string is kept in a file, you can use *if=* to specify the full pathname of the file, just as in *termcap*. By practice, *if=* (and *rf=*) are used when the tab setting commands get impractically long. This is the case for just a few terminals. The files are usually kept in the directory */usr/lib/tabset*. It is generally good practice to avoid them. You may use the *iprog=* capability to enter the full pathname of an initialization program to be run.

When the user logs in, the capabilities are used in the following order: The program specified by *iprog=* is run first, and then the *is1=* and *is2=* strings are sent. The margins are next set using *mgc=*, *smgl=*, and *smgr=*. Then the tabs are set using *hts=* and *tbc=*, the string kept in the file specified by *if=* is sent, and finally the *is3=* string is sent.

- *The Reset Capabilities:*
  There are four *terminfo* reset capabilities: *rs1=*, *rs2=*, *rs3=* and *rf=*. They are parallel to the *is1=*, *is2=*, *is3=* and *if=* *terminfo* initialization capabilities.

  Although officially, **r2=** is the *termcap* equivalent of *rs2=*, *captoinfo* is tolerant and will translate either **r2=** or **rs=** into *rs2=*.

  The reset capabilities should be powerful enough to reset the terminal from a totally unknown state. They usually contain the initialization commands, plus commands that would be unnecessary and annoying when logging in, such as setting the DEC vt100 to 80 columns, but might be needed to get you out of a jam. If the terminal has a RESET button, the characters that it sends might be just what you need.

  In System V, the reset strings are output by *tput reset*, which is used when the terminal is wedged.

Although there are *termcap* equivalents to the *terminfo* initialization and reset capabilities, they are included only to allow consistency between the two systems. If you have a *termcap* system, you should not be using **i1=**, **i3=**, **r1=** or **r3=** because, in all likelihood, they are not being used.

PROGRAM INITIALIZATION

Terminfo	*Termcap*	*Description*
smcup=	**ti=**	Initialization for programs that use cursor motion.
rmcup=	**te=**	End programs that use cursor motion.
nrrmc	**NR**	*smcup=* does not reverse *rmcup=* (*terminfo* only).

The traditional definition of the program initialization capabilities is that there is one capability to initialize programs that will perform cursor motion and another for when that program finishes. This definition is used by older *termcap* systems and by *terminfo*.

There are two reasons why you may want to include the program initialization capabilities in your entry. First, some terminals allow the cursor movement command to be turned on and off. One advantage of turning cursor movement off when it is not needed is that it prevents the cursor movement commands from being given accidentally. Second, some terminals, like the Concept, have more than one page of memory. If such a multi-page terminal has only memory-relative cursor addressing, then you will want to fix a single screen sized page of the memory in the screen so that you can use absolute cursor movement.

Some terminals (e.g., Tektronix 4025) have multiple or programmable command characters, and the terminal initialization capability can fix the command character to the one used in the capability descriptions.

In BSD 4.3 *termcap*, however, that definition has been broadened so that **ti=**, the *termcap* initialization capability, is used to initialize all programs that use *termcap*, and **te=** is used when programs finish. Fortunately, *termcap* entries and programs should be compatible in both directions. The best plan is to follow the convention of your particular system and be alert to the difference when porting programs or entries, but do not worry excessively about it unless problems arise.

If you are using an *xterm* terminal emulation window, you can disable the **ti=** and **te=** capabilities by setting the *titeInhibit* resource for the *xterm* client. See *The X Window System User's Guide* for more information on the X Window System, *xterm*, and setting resource variables.

The *nrrmc* capability is a simple Boolean flag that indicates that the *smcup=* string will not restore the screen after the *rmcup=* string is output. Few terminal entries specify this capability, and its *termcap* equivalent, **NR**, is not included in BSD 4.3 *termcap*.

SETTING AND USING TABS

Terminfo	Termcap	Description
hts=	st=	Set a tab stop in all rows, current column.
tbc=	ct=	Clear all tab stops.
it#	it#	Initial number of spaces between tabs.
ht=	ta=	Tab: move to next hardware tab stop (usually ^I).
cbt=	bt=	Back tab: move to previous tab stop.
	pt	Perform tabs: terminal has hardware tabs (obsolete).

All the capabilities in this section describe "hardware tabs," that is, tabs that are performed by the actual terminal hardware. You should make a distinction between these and software tabs, which are translated into the right number of spaces by UNIX before being sent to the terminal.

By convention, if the terminal is set to use software tabs, then programs should not use the the following capabilities because the tab stops may not be properly set.

- *Setting and Clearing Tabs:*
  The tab set and tab clear capabilities are straightforward. The tab set capability, **st=** in *termcap* and *hts=* in *terminfo*, sets a hardware tab in every row at the column the cursor is in. If a complicated sequence is needed to set tabs, consider including it in the initialization capabilities described in the previous section. While this deprives programs of the ability to set tabs dynamically, hardware tabs regularly spaced eight spaces apart usually suffice. Specify the string for clearing all hardware tabs in the **ct=** capability in *termcap* or the *tbc=* capability in *terminfo*.

- *Distance Between Tabs:*
  Some terminals set their hardware tabs automatically when they are powered up. If so, specify the distance between tabs with the **it#** capability in both *termcap* and *terminfo*. For most such terminals, the setting will be 8.

This information is used by *tset* (BSD 4.3) or *tput init* (System V) to determine whether to set the driver modes to hardware tab expansion and whether to set the tab stops. If **it#** is set to 8, then the tabs are already properly set. If it is set to anything but 8, the hardware tabs should be reset so that they are 8 apart if they can. If they cannot be reset, then the terminal driver should be set up so that it converts all tabs to the correct number of spaces.

There is no way to specify the initial tab setup if it is anything more complex than regular spacing across the screen. If a terminal has some irregular hardware tab arrangement when powered on, the tabs should be cleared and reset and you should make sure that **it#** is not set to 8.

UNIX assumes that tab stops are set eight spaces apart. Most terminals must have their tab stops initialized. See the initialization capabilities for more information on setting them upon startup.

- *Tab Character:*
  The command string to move the cursor to the next hardware tab stop should be placed in the **ta=** capability in *termcap* and the **ht=** capability in *terminfo*. On almost every terminal, this command will be ^I. You should, however, take this opportunity to include padding information if your terminal needs a delay.

If your system is using software tabs, you should be careful that programs do not use the hardware tabs either with this capability or with the back tab capability described below.

- *Backwards Tabs:*
  For moving backwards to the previous tab stop, the **bt=** (*termcap*) or *cbt=* (*terminfo*) capability can be used. Consult your terminal reference manual to see if your terminal has backward tabs. Many terminals do not have a backwards tab, and few programs depend on it, so it is not too important. As mentioned above, programs should not use the **bt=** (or **ta=**) capabilities if the system is using software tabs. Some padding may be necessary.

- *Performing Hardware Tabs (obsolete):*
  The *termcap* **pt** capability is obsolete, meaning that it does not have a *terminfo* equivalent. It is simply a Boolean capability set for terminals that can perform hardware tabs. In the past, *termcap* would use either the **pt** or the **ta=** capability to indicate that the terminal could perform hardware tabs. If **pt** was specified, the **ta=** capability could be omitted, and it would be assumed to be ^I with no padding necessary. *terminfo* does not use the **pt** capability (or any equivalent) because of its redundancy but instead requires that the *ht=* capability be specified if the terminal can perform hardware tabs.

  We describe **pt** here because it is a part of BSD 4.3, and for backward capability with older UNIX systems and programs that depend on them. However, new programs should not use **pt** but instead should follow the *terminfo* conventions and specify the tab stop capability for every terminal that can perform hardware tabs.

See Chapter 14 for information on the destructive tab glitch.

MARGINS

Terminfo	Termcap	Description
smgl=	ML=	Set left soft margin (not in BSD 4.3).
smgr=	MR=	Set right soft margin (not in BSD 4.3).
mgc=	MC=	Clear soft margins (not in BSD 4.3).
smam=	SA=	Turn on automatic margins (not in BSD 4.3).
rmam=	RA=	Turn off automatic margins (not in BSD 4.3).

Soft margins are a new *terminfo* feature that are not a part of BSD 4.3 *termcap*. They are margins that are used instead of the normal left and right hard terminal margins. These capabilities are largely self-explanatory; however, you should note that the capabilities to set the left and right margins do not take parameters, so the margins can be set to only one place.

- *Setting Left and Right Soft Margins:*
  In *terminfo*, the string for setting the left soft margin should be placed in the *smgl=* capability and the string for setting the right soft margin should be in the *smgr=* capability. The *termcap* equivalent for these capabilities are, respectively, **ML=** and **MR=**.

- *Clearing Soft Margins:*
  The string to clear any soft margins should be set in the *mgc=* capability in *terminfo*, or with the **MC=** capability in *termcap*.

- *Turning On and Off Automatic Soft Margins:*
  If automatic margins can be turned on and off, specify the strings in the *smam=* and *rmam=* capabilities in *terminfo*, and in the **SA=** and **RA=** capabilities in *termcap*. (See the **am** automargin capability described in Chapter 16).

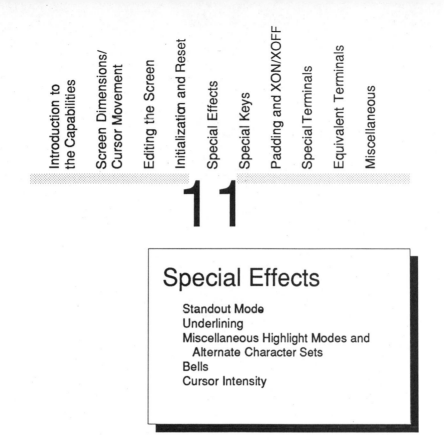

Introduction to
the Capabilities

Screen Dimensions/
Cursor Movement

Editing the Screen

Initialization and Reset

Special Effects

Special Keys

Padding and XON/XOFF

Special Terminals

Equivalent Terminals

Miscellaneous

11

Special Effects

Standout Mode
Underlining
Miscellaneous Highlight Modes and
    Alternate Character Sets
Bells
Cursor Intensity

This chapter covers terminal effects meant to capture the user's attention. Included in this category are highlight modes, alternate character sets, and audio and visual bells.

In general, programs will be able to operate terminals without standout, underline, or any of the other special display options. However, if your terminal does have these features, you should include them in the database entry so that they can be used—every little enhancement counts.

133

STANDOUT
MODE

Terminfo	*Termcap*	*Description*
smso=	so=	Begin standout mode.
rmso=	se=	End standout mode.
xmc#	sg#	Standout glitch: number of spaces printed when change to standout mode (default is 0).
msgr	ms	Move safe: can move cursor gracefully in standout or underline mode.

Many terminals can highlight characters in several different ways, such as bright, dim, flashing, etc. Some do it by altering intensity, others by going to reverse video. You can specify one such mode as "standout mode," which will be used by programs as a general purpose highlighting mechanism. The important point is that you get to designate which terminal display mode is standout mode: the terminal probably does not have one pre-arranged.

- *Choosing the Standout Mode:*
  Choosing the standout mode is important, because many programs use it. Fewer programs specifically select underline and alternate character sets, and even fewer use the other highlight modes because they are not widely available. Standout mode should be the most distinctive mode your terminal has. In general, reverse video is a better choice than extra bright. Flashing is very prominent but also somewhat disruptive. Consult your terminal manual to find the possible highlight modes and experiment with them until you find the one that seems most effective for your terminal. You can easily test your standout mode by using *cat*, printing the standout string, then some characters, then the standout end string.

  Use the chosen command sequences in the **so=** (standout start) and **se=** (standout end) string capabilities in *termcap*, and *smso=* and *rmso=* in *terminfo*.

- *Magic Cookies:*
  Some terminals unavoidably print one or more spaces when they enter and leave standout mode. These are called "magic cookies". Other terminals implement special modes by storing extra data with each character and do not need magic cookies. The sg# capability in *termcap* and the **xmc#** capability in *terminfo* is specified for terminals that leave magic cookies when going into standout mode. The glitch field contains the number of spaces that are sent when switching to or from standout mode. *termcap* and *terminfo* assume that the magic cookie for turning on standout mode is the same length as the magic cookie for turning off standout mode.

What should you do if the magic cookie for switching into standout mode does not match the one for switching out? Set the glitch to the larger number and add extra spaces to the capability with the shorter magic cookie. In this way, the magic cookies have artificially been made equal, and the glitch capability can account for both. (For example, if a terminal uses a two-space magic cookie when turning standout on and a one-space magic cookie when turning standout off, add an extra space to the end of the "standout end" capability and set the glitch capability to two.)

To keep *termcap* or *terminfo* entries from being unnecessarily long, you should not include **sg#0** if your terminal does not have a standout glitch. Zero (0) will be set as a default value automatically. Most terminals do not have the standout glitch.

terminfo and *termcap* handle the standout and underline glitches differently. *termcap* has the sg# capability for standout magic cookies, **ug#** for underline magic cookies, and no specifically defined capabilities for magic cookies in the other highlight capabilities. In most cases, sg# and ug# are identical, and there are similar glitches for other highlight modes. In contrast, *terminfo* has a single capability called **xmc#** to describe the magic cookies for standout, underline, and any other special mode. (By definition, the *terminfo* **xmc#** capability is analogous to the *termcap* sg# capability, and the *termcap* **ug#** capability has no *terminfo* pair. Thus, *captoinfo* will ignore ug#.) In most cases, the simpler *terminfo* system is preferable because the modes are usually identical, and if not, a trick similar to the one described above can be engineered.

• *Moving Safely in Standout Mode:*
Most terminals cannot move the cursor properly while in standout or underline mode: they may leave a trail of standout or underlined characters behind them if they are given a cursor move instruction. Other terminals turn the special mode off. Some terminals are smarter and do move properly within standout mode, and these terminals are given the "move safe" capability in standout mode, represented by the Boolean capability **ms** in *termcap*, or *msgr* in *terminfo*. If this capability is not present, the assumption is that the terminal cannot move properly in an enhanced video mode, so the program must compensate by switching to normal mode, moving, and then returning to standout mode.

Some terminals automatically turn off standout mode when they start a new line. Some do not. This feature seems like a natural candidate for a Boolean capability, but no such capability has been defined. Instead, the convention is that programs always turn off standout mode before they send a new line to the terminal. The system manager who is writing a new entry can relax, while programmers must make sure they follow the convention.

UNDERLINING

Terminfo	Termcap	Description
smul=	us=	Begin underline mode.
rmul=	ue=	End underline mode.
uc=	uc=	Underline character at cursor, move cursor right.
	ug#	Underline glitch: number of spaces printed when change to underline mode. Only set if non-zero (not in *terminfo*).
ul	ul	Terminal underlines even though it cannot overstrike.

- *Entering and Leaving Underline Mode:*
  The underlining capabilities correspond to the standout capabilities. Underline start (**us=** in *termcap* and **smul=** in *terminfo*) works the same as the standout start capability in placing the terminal into underline mode. Underline end (**ue=** in *termcap* and **rmul=** in *terminfo*) works similarly to the standout end capability and ends underline mode.

- *Underlining a Character:*
  The underline character capability (**uc=** in both *termcap* and *terminfo*) has no standout equivalent: it underlines the character the cursor is on and moves the cursor one space to the right. It is mostly for older terminals which do not have a proper underline mode.

- *Underline Glitch:*
  In *termcap*, the underline glitch capability, **ug#**, works just like sg#: it is the number of spaces the terminal moves when switching to or from underline mode. In *terminfo*, this capability has no official equivalent; the **xmc#** glitch capability, however, covers the underline glitch as well as the standout glitch and acts as a functional equivalent. Since it is officially the analog to sg#, it is covered in the standout section of this chapter.

- *Underlining Without Overstrike:*
  Some terminals underline by typing a character, backspacing, and typing an underscore. This requires a terminal that can overstrike—that is, can type one character on top of another so that both show. (See the **os** overstrike capability.) Other terminals can underline in this way even though they cannot overstrike in general. For either of these terminal types, specify the **ul** capability. In general, hardcopy terminals underline by overstriking, but video terminals use an alternate character set.

- *Moving Safely in Underline Mode:*
  The "move safe" capability described in the standout section of this chapter also applies to underlines.

MISCELLANEOUS HIGHLIGHT MODES AND ALTERNATE CHARACTER SETS

Terminfo	Termcap	Description
rev=	mr=	Turn on reverse video attribute.
blink=	mb=	Turn on blinking attribute.
bold=	md=	Turn on bold (extra-bright) attribute.
dim=	mh=	Turn on dim (half-bright) attribute.
invis=	mk=	Turn on blanking attribute (characters invisible).
prot=	mp=	Turn on protected attribute.
smacs=	as=	Start using alternate character set.
rmacs=	ae=	End using alternate character set.
enacs=	eA=	Enable alternate character set (not in BSD 4.3).
sgr0=	me=	Turn off all attributes (including alternate character set).
sgr=	sa=	Set #1 #2 #3 #4 #5 #6 #7 #8 #9 attributes (mainly *terminfo*).

Standout and underline are the most important display modes. Standout mode is particularly important, because it is used by many programs. However in addition to standout and underline, some terminals provide the capabilities for additional special display modes. There are nine modes in all: standout and underline, reverse, blinking, bold, dim, blanking (invisible text), protected (where the terminal "protects" the text from overwriting or erasing in a terminal-dependent way), and alternate character set.

- *Other Highlight Modes:*
  The first six capabilities listed in this section describe the string to turn on their respective modes. Some of these modes are mutually exclusive, such as dim and bold, while others may not be. The relationship between the various modes remains undefined in *termcap* and *terminfo*, since it varies by terminal and by mode. You will

have to experiment with your terminal to learn whether turning on one mode turns off others.

- *Alternate Character Sets:*
Terminals may have complete, software-selectable alternate character sets, such as Greek or Italic or graphic character sets. (This is not the same as terminals that, if loaded with the right ROMs, have international versions—sending "£" instead of "#" for shift 3— since those terminals are configured by the hardware.) Not many programs use alternate character sets.

Although your terminal may support several alternate character sets, there is space for only one alternate character set command. For these terminals, you could create several database entries for the terminal, each using a different alternate character set.

Entering and Leaving Alternate Character Sets:
Alternate character sets, like underline and standout and unlike the other six display modes, are entered by sending one character string, and left by sending another. In *termcap*, these character strings should be entered in **as=** for alternate start and **ae=** for alternate end. In *terminfo*, the equivalent capabilities are **smacs=** (to start) and **rmacs** (to end). Some padding may be required.

Enabling Alternate Character Sets:
Some terminals need to enable the alternate character set before they can start using it. In *terminfo*, you may place the string to enable alternate character sets in the **enacs=** capability. The AT&T recommended *termcap* equivalent is **eA=**, but it is not a part of BSD 4.3 *termcap* nor of older *termcap* systems.

- *Turning Off All Modes:*
To turn off all special modes, specify the **me=** capability in *termcap* or the **sgr0=** capability in *terminfo*. This capability should turn off standout and underline as well and alternate character set. Some padding may be required.

- *Setting All Attributes in One Capability:*
The *terminfo* **sgr=** capability is the most complicated capability. It uses **nine** parameters, one for each possible mode! In theory, the **sgr=** capability specifies how to turn on an arbitrary combination of the nine modes (if the nth parameter is set to 1, the nth mode is turned on; if the nth parameter is 0, the mode is turned off). The *termcap* equivalent to **sgr=** is **sa=**, but in practice, this capability

requires elaborate syntax and is better suited to *terminfo* than *term-cap*. Consequently, it is expected that few *termcap* programs will attempt to use the **sa=** capability. It is a part of the official BSD 4.3 *termcap*, but only for compatibility with *terminfo*.

This lack affects both programmers and database entry writers. Programs must be prepared for either case. Programs can force all other attributes off before setting the desired mode, and this is probably the best convention as it is the most controlled. On systems where this capability is implemented, programs can use it to try to set a combination of modes, although the terminal hardware may be unable to go into the requested combination of modes. Database entry writers, who have terminals that can go into some modes simultaneously, must decide how they want their terminal to behave.

The remainder of this section provides an excellent example of setting attributes with *sgr=*. The example is adapted from the AT&T System V documentation.

Example of *sgr=* (Terminfo Set All) Capability

Consider a terminal that uses the following escape sequences for attributes:

Parameter	Attribute	Escape Sequence
	none	\E[0m
p1	standout	\E[0;4;7m
p2	underline	\E[0;3m
p3	reverse	\E[0;4m
p4	blink	\E[0;5m
p5	dim	\E[0;7m
p6	bold	\E[0;3;4m
p7	invis	\E[0;8m
p8	protect	Not available on this terminal
p9	altcharset	^O (off) ^N(on)

Each escape sequence gives the 0 to turn off modes before giving the digit to turn on the desired mode. Standout mode is set to whatever we feel stands out the best; here it is set as the combination of reverse and dim. We assume that this terminal does not have a true bold mode, so bold is set as the combination of reverse and underline. If a terminal does not have a mode and has no way to simulate it (as with the protected mode in this example), then it is simply omitted. This example terminal treats the alternate character set (*altcharset*) differently from the other attributes: The sequence to turn on the *altcharset* mode on is ^N and the sequence to turn it off is ^O.

The sequence to turn all modes on would be:

```
\E[0;3;4;5;7;8m^N
```

Now we need to transform the table so that one column is the escape codes and the other is which parameters it should be used with. For example, ;3 should be output when either underline (the p2 parameter) or bold (the p6 parameter) is requested. The complete table is:

Sequence	When To Output	Terminfo Translation
\E[0	always	\E[0
;3	if p2 or p6	%?%p2%p6%l%t;3%;
;4	if p1 or p3 or p6	%?%p1%p3%l%p6%l%t;4%;
;5	if p4	%?%p4%t;5%;
;7	if p1 or p5	%?%p1%p5%l%t;7%;
;8	if p7	%?%p7%t;8%;
m	always	m
^N or ^O	if p9 ^N, else ^O	%?%p9%t^N%e^O%;

The *sgr=* capability is formed by concatenating all these sequences together.

```
sgr=\E[0%?%p2%p6%|%t;3%;%?%p1%p3%|%p6%|%t;4%;%?%p5%t
    ;5%;%?%p1%p5%|%t;7%;%?%p7%t;8%;m%?%p9%t^N%e^O%;,
```

BELLS

Terminfo	Termcap	Description
flash=	**vb=**	Visual bell: flash terminal screen.
bel=	**bl=**	Audio bell: make terminal noise. Usually ^G.

- *Visual Bells:*
  A visual bell is one which flashes the screen without moving the cursor, thus drawing the attention of the user without annoying all nearby colleagues. The string for this bell should be placed in the *flash=* capability in *terminfo*, and in the **vb=** capability in *termcap*.

  This capability is often created by switching back and forth between reverse and normal video modes for the entire screen, with mandatory padding in between. For example, if \EX goes into reverse video and \EY returns to normal video, a suitable *terminfo* entry might be:

  ```
  flash = \EX$<500/>\EY$<500/>\EX$<500/>\EY,
  ```

  Note that this cannot be done in *termcap* because all of the padding is done once, at the end of the sequence. All one would see is a brief flicker followed by a pause.

- *Audio Bells:*
  An audio bell will make the terminal beep, buzz, ring, squeak or generally make some sort of noise. The command is ^G on most terminals. This string should be placed in the *bel=* capability in *terminfo*, and in the **bl=** capability in *termcap*.

CURSOR
INTENSITY

Terminfo	Termcap	Description
cvvis=	vs=	Make cursor very visible.
civis=	vi=	Make cursor invisible.
cnorm=	ve=	Make cursor normal (undo effect of vs= and vi).
chts	HC	Cursor hard to see when not on bottom line (not in BSD 4.3).

- *Cursor Visibility:*
  When visual mode was added to the *vi* editor, two *termcap* capabilities were added: **vs=** (visual start) was output whenever *vi* went into visual mode, and **ve=** was output whenever *vi* left visual mode. There was considerable confusion between these capabilities and the **ti=** (*smcup=*) and **te=** (*rmcup=*) capabilities (q.v.).

When *terminfo* was being created, the **vs=/ve=** capabilities were examined, and it was discerned that their primary use was to change the cursor setting to something more visible. The few *termcap* entries that did otherwise were rewritten, moving the other sequences to **ti=** and **te=**. The capabilities were subsequently renamed to reflect this evolution in their definition.

vs= (*cvvis=*) makes the cursor very visible (such as a flashing block instead of an underline); this capability should be used when the cursor is hard to see. **ve=** (*cnorm=*) returns the cursor to a normal mode. The capability **vi=** (*civis=*) was also added for specifying the sequence to make the cursor invisible. BSD 4.3 *termcap* follows these conventions.

To find out how your system treats these capabilities, look up *termcap* in your own system specific manual or try the strings manually and see what they do. New programs should assume that these capabilities are limited to changing the cursor so that they will be upwardly compatible with *terminfo*. Similarly, new *termcap* entries should also follow the new, more limited convention, even on older systems. Be sure to check these capabilities when copying a *termcap* capability from an older system to a BSD 4.3 system or when converting to *terminfo*.

* *If the Cursor is Hard to See:*
  If the cursor is hard to see when it is not on the bottom line, you should specify the *chts* capability in *terminfo*. This can be used as a hint to the program to make the cursor very visible. For example, a non-flashing underline can be hard to find in the middle of a page of text. Although there is a *termcap* equivalent (**HC**), *chts* is essentially a *terminfo* capability that is not in BSD 4.3 *termcap* or older *termcap* systems.

Introduction to the Capabilities

Screen Dimensions/ Cursor Movement

Editing the Screen

Initialization and Reset

Special Effects

Special Keys

Padding and XON/XOFF

Special Terminals

Equivalent Terminals

Miscellaneous

12

Special Keys

Special Function Keys
Extended Function Key Definitions
Programmable Function Keys
Keypad Keys
Other Special Keyboard Keys
Extended Special Key Descriptions
Non-Standard Control Characters

There are two types of keys discussed in this chapter: straightforward function keys (for which the capability strings are simply assigned the string the key outputs) and *programmable* function keys. Programmable keys are keys which a program may use to perform a more complex function.

For the standard function keys, writing a capability string just involves finding out what string the key sends (from the terminal manual or using the methods described in Chapter 5) and placing that sequence in the string definition. This will allow programs to know which key has been pressed and act accordingly.

SPECIAL FUNCTION KEYS

Terminfo	Termcap	Description
kf0=	k0=	The string sent by the zeroth function key (labeled f10).
kf1=	k1=	The string sent by the first function key (labeled f1).
kf2=	k2=	The string sent by the second function key (labeled f2).
... *kf9*=	... k9=	The string sent by the ninth function key (labeled f9).
lf0=	l0=	The label on the zeroth function key if not F10.
lf1=	l1=	The label on the first function key if not F1.
lf2=	l2=	The label on the second function key if not F2.
... *lf9*=	... l9=	The label on the ninth function key if not F9.
	kn#	The number of function keys defined.

terminfo and *termcap* allow for up to 64 function keys. The first ten are the most significant and will be discussed first.

- *The Function Keys:*
  The *kfn*= capabilities in *terminfo* and the k*n*= capabilities in *termcap* are designed to hold the sequence sent by the corresponding function key. Once the function keys are defined by these capabilities, they can be used in the *vi* :**map** command. The :**map** command allows the *n*th function key to be referred to as "#*n*", so the *vi* command ":map #6 *string*" will cause *vi* to execute the command sequence specified by *string* when the sixth function key is

pressed. The function keys must be defined with capabilities so that the mapping can be terminal independent.

In addition, *terminfo* has capabilities for programming these function keys from an application program. These capabilities are discussed at the end of this chapter.

If you are using BSD 4.3 *termcap*, a logistics problem comes up with terminals (such as the Wyse-50) that label their function keys starting at F1 rather than F0. For these terminals, you should define the **k0=** capability for the key labeled "f10" and allow the rest of the capabilities to correspond to the numbered function keys, since BSD 4.3 *termcap* only allows ten function keys to be defined.

You may use a keyboard start and keyboard end sequence to activate and deactivate your keyboard. If so, specify these in the **ks=** and **ke=** capabilities in *termcap*, or the **smkx=** and **rmkx=** capabilities in *terminfo*, described elsewhere in this chapter.

- *Labeling Function Keys:*
  Some terminals have function keys labeled something other than "F0" through "F9". For example, the Heathkit h-19 has function keys labeled "blue", "red", and "white". The **l0=** through **l9=** capabilities are used to hold the labels for function keys if those labels are something other than the usual "F0" through "F9". The values sent by those function keys must also be defined. For example, the entry for the Heathkit h-19 in our sample */etc/termcap* contains the line:

  ```
  :16=blue:17=red:18=white:k6=\EP:k7=\EQ:k8=\ER
  ```

  This allows programs to give more useful error messages. The labeling capabilities are rarely needed.

- *Number of Function Keys:*
  In older versions of *termcap*, the **kn#** capability should be set to contain the number of special function keys (provided it is not 0). This does not include the arrow keys and named keys. Due to its irregular use in *termcap*, and the extended function key capabilities in *terminfo*, *terminfo* does not define an equivalent capability to **kn#**. Therefore, **kn#** is considered "obsolete" in BSD 4.3 *termcap*.

EXTENDED FUNCTION KEY DEFINITIONS

Terminfo	Termcap	Description
kf10=	k;=	The string sent by the eleventh function key (labeled f10).
kf11=	F1=	The string sent by function key f11.
kf12=	F2=	The string sent by function key f12.
kf13=	F3=	The string sent by function key f13.
...	...	
kf19=	F9=	The string sent by function key f19.
kf20=	FA=	The string sent by function key f20.
kf21=	FB=	The string sent by function key f21.
kf22=	FC=	The string sent by function key f22.
...	...	
kf44=	FY=	The string sent by function key f44.
kf45=	FZ=	The string sent by function key f45.
kf46=	Fa=	The string sent by function key f46.
kf47=	Fb=	The string sent by function key f47.
kf48=	Fc=	The string sent by function key f48.
...	...	
kf62=	Fq=	The string sent by function key f62.
kf63=	Fr=	The string sent by function key f63.
lf10=	la=	The eleventh function key label.

terminfo extends the function keys capabilities from the original ten described above to a full 64. Although there are suggested equivalences for *termcap* listed above, BSD 4.3 *termcap* does not actually support these extended keys.

The label for the eleventh function key is defined in the **la=** capability in *termcap* and the *lf10* capability in *terminfo*. The "a" in **la=** is used because it is the hex representation of ten. See the description of function label keys in the previous section.

PROGRAMMABLE FUNCTION KEYS

Terminfo	Termcap	Description
pfkey=	pk=	Program key #1 to treat string #2 as if typed by user (mainly *terminfo*).
pfloc=	pl=	Program key #1 to execute string #2 in local mode (mainly *terminfo*).
pfx=	px=	Program key #1 to transmit string #2 to computer (mainly *terminfo*).
pln=	pn=	Program soft label #1 to show string #2 (not in BSD 4.3).
smln=	LO=	Turn soft labels on (not in BSD 4.3).
rmln=	LF=	Turn soft labels off (not in BSD 4.3).
nlab#	Nl#	Number of soft labels available (not in BSD 4.3).
lw#	lw#	Width (number of columns) in each soft label (not in BSD 4.3).
lh#	lh#	Height (number of rows) in each soft label (not in BSD 4.3).

In distinction to a standard function key, which always generates a fixed string (or, at best, a string defined in the terminal's setup mode), a programmable function key can be programmed to generate different strings at different points in a program.

Capabilities thus exist for parameterized programming of function keys, as well as for defining on-screen "soft" labels for the keys.

The programming capabilities are primarily for *terminfo*. Since *termcap* has no way to indicate a string as a parameter, it cannot implement **pk=**, **pl=**, **px=** and **pn=**. These capabilities are assigned *termcap* definitions solely for programs that are converting between *termcap* and *terminfo*. It is also possible that some future version of *termcap* will implement strings as parameters. The programming capabilities are defined in BSD 4.3 *termcap* but not implemented. (The soft label capabilities are not even defined in BSD 4.3.)

- *Programming a Function Key:*
  Up to 11 function keys can be programmed with the first three capabilities listed above. The programming capabilities take two run time parameters: the first to say which function key to program, the second to say what string that key should generate.

  The first parameter is the function key number in the range 0 to 10. (Some terminals have more than 11 programmable function keys, but at present, programming those extra keys is not supported.) The second parameter is a string. The three programming capabilities differ in how they program the function key to issue that string.

  a. The first programming capability listed above says to interpret the key as if the string were typed by the user. Usually, this means that the string is sent to the computer, which interprets it and echoes it back to the screen. This capability is called *pfkey=* in *terminfo* and **pk=** in *termcap*.

  b. The second capability, called *pfloc=* in *terminfo* and **pl=** in *termcap*, says to interpret the key as if the string were typed on the keyboard in local mode.

  c. The third capability, *pfx=* in *terminfo* and **px=** in *termcap*, says to send the given string directly to the computer when the specified key is pressed.

- *Soft Labels:*
  The programmable function keys may have soft labels, which are small blocks of text describing the function key, usually displayed in standout mode in a row at the top or bottom of the screen. A soft label may be programmed to show a particular string with the **pn=** capability in *termcap*, or the *pln=* capability in *terminfo*. Like the other three programming capabilities discussed above, this capability takes two parameters, the key number (0 to 11) to be programmed and the string to program it with.

- *Turning On and Off Soft Labels:*
  Soft labels may be turned on and off with the *smln=* and *rmln=* capabilities in *terminfo* and the **LO=** and **LF=** capabilities in *termcap*. Programs that change a soft label with **pn=** or *pln=* should then send the **LO=** or *smln=* string, because not all terminals update the soft labels automatically when they are changed.

- *Number, Height and Width of Soft Labels:*
  The number of soft labels are defined in the **Nl#** capability in *termcap* and the **nlab#** capability in *terminfo*. The width and height of the box used by the terminal to display a soft label can be declared with the **lw#** and **lh#** capabilities in both *termcap* and *terminfo*, with the width measured in columns and the height in rows. All three of these capabilities may require padding.

KEYPAD
KEYS

Terminfo	Termcap	Description
kcuu1=	ku=	Sent by up arrow key (corresponds to *cuu1=* and up=).
kcub1=	kl=	Sent by left arrow key (corresponds to bc= or bs).
kcuf1=	kr=	Sent by right arrow key (corresponds to *cuf1=* and nd=).
kcud1=	kd=	Sent by down arrow key (corresponds to *cud1=* and do=).
khome=	kh=	Sent by the home key (corresponds to *home=* and ho=).
ka1=	K1=	Sent by upper left key of keypad.
kb2=	K2=	Sent by upper right key of keypad.
ka3=	K3=	Sent by center key of keypad.
kc1=	K4=	Sent by lower left key of keypad.
kc3=	K5=	Sent by lower right key of keypad.
smkx=	ks=	Turn keypad on, if can be turned on and off.
rmkx=	ke=	Turn keypad off, if can be turned on and off.
	ma=	Map keypad to cursor movement for *vi* version 2.

Many terminals have arrow keypads that transmit character sequences to move the cursor. These keypads are often arranged as a 3x3 matrix, consisting of the four arrow keys and five other keys in the keypad (at the four corners and the center). The home key is considered part of the keypad by some terminals, so it is included here.

The easiest way to find out the sequences sent by the arrow and cursor movement keys is to look them up in your terminal manual. However, there are several on-line techniques you can use if your manual is lost or unavailable. These techniques are described in Chapter 5.

- *Turning the Keypad On and Off:*
  On some terminals the keypad can be turned on and off by sending
  a command sequence. The command sequences to enable (start)
  and disable (end) the keypad are given in the **ks=** and **ke=** capabilities in *termcap*, and in the *smkx=* and *rmkx=* capabilities in *terminfo*. If these capabilities are not given, the keypad is assumed
  always to be on.

  The terminal decides what keys it considers as part of the keypad.
  See your terminal manual for this information.

- *The Map Capability:*
  The **ma=** keypad map capability is officially obsolete. It was used
  by *vi* version 2 to map the sequences sent by arrow keys to the cursor movement commands in *vi*. That is now done with the arrow
  and home capabilities instead. While **ma=** is obsolete, it is still
  included in some *termcap* entries, and some programs may still
  depend on it. If you are writing a new *termcap* entry, include **ma=**
  if you have software that needs it. If you are writing a new program, do not use the **ma=** capability, because it is no longer supported.

  The syntax for the **ma=** capability is to list the sequence sent by an
  arrow key before the corresponding cursor movement command in
  vi. Those *vi* cursor movement commands are: up=**j**, down=**k**,
  left=**h**, right=**l**, and home=**H**. Therefore, if you have keypad capabilities in *termcap* of ku=^Z, kd=^K, kl=^H, kr=^X, and
  kh=^L, the equivalent map capability would be:

  ```
  ma=^Zj^Kk^Hh^Xl^LH
  ```

  If the keypad is missing one or more keys, they are omitted from
  the **ma=** capability along with the *vi* cursor movement command to
  which they correspond. Therefore, for a terminal with only a
  HOME key which sends ^L, ma=^LH would be correct.

OTHER SPECIAL
KEYBOARD KEYS

Terminfo	Termcap	Description
kll=	kH=	String sent by **home-down** (to lower left).
kbs=	kb=	String sent by **backspace**.
ktbc=	ka=	String sent by **clear all tabs**.
kctab=	kt=	String sent by **clear tab** (in this column only).
kcbt=	kB=	String sent by **back tab** (not in BSD 4.3).
kclr=	kC=	String sent by **clear screen** or **erase**.
kdch1=	kD=	String sent by **delete character**.
kdll=	kL=	String sent by **delete line**.
krmir=	kM=	String sent by **exit insert mode**.
kel=	kE=	String sent by **clear to end of line**.
ked=	kS=	String sent by **clear to end of screen**.
kich1=	kI=	String sent by **insert character** or **enter insert mode**.
kill=	kA=	String sent by **insert line**.
knp=	kN=	String sent by **next page**.
kpp=	kP=	String sent by **previous page**.
kind=	kF=	String sent by **scroll forward/down**.
kri=	kR=	String sent by **scroll backwards/up**.
khts=	kT=	String sent by **set tab stop** (in this column).
	ko=	"Keys other": lists the cursor movement capabilities for which there is a defined key.

With the exception of **ko=**, the capabilities in this section are straight-forward. They each describe the special character(s) sent by a key on the keyboard, which you can determine either by reading the manufacturer's terminal handbook or by testing the keys directly.

Few terminals will have all of these keys. Simply specify the ones that are available and ignore the rest.

With the exception of **kb=**, these capabilities are relatively new additions to *termcap*, coming into use with *terminfo* around 1986. Older UNIX systems probably will not use these capabilities and may flag them as unknown. Older programs will ignore them. However, not listing a key may cause serious problems while running a program if the unlisted key were accidentally hit. The program will not be able to translate the sequence into a recognizable function key sequence and will be forced to interpret the sequence as if the characters had been typed, which may be disastrous.

Many of these capabilities have "twin" capabilities elsewhere in *termcap* and *terminfo*. For example, in *termcap*, **kC=** specifies the code sent by the CLEAR SCREEN key, and **cl=** is the string that programs use to clear the screen. The capabilities in this section describe what is sent when a key is pressed, so that programs know what special keys are available and to realize when one has been pressed. The twin capabilities for each of these keys (described elsewhere in this book) are the functional capabilities, which is how programs learn what strings to send to produce the desired action.

Although in most cases the twins will be identical twins, there are a few reasons and special cases where the twins will not be identical. You might want to specify padding for the functional capabilities. Or you might want to remap the keyboard (for example, by putting a template over it) or use the keys to indicate something other than they say on them (for example, using the arrow keys for something other than moving the cursor in application programs.) In these cases, your program would turn off echoing and watch the input for the characters sent by the redefined keys. As another, somewhat far-fetched example, you might use the keyboard of one terminal to control the screen of another and so would have to translate the characters sent by the keystroke on the first terminal to their functional equivalents on the other. Thus, while it is often redundant to have twin capabilities, there are cases when it is useful, and it is historically ingrained. The safest course is to provide both capabilities and use them to check each other.

Note that your terminal may be able to perform a command without having a key defined on the keyboard for it. For example, most terminals have a clear command, but many do not have clear keys on their keyboards.

Note that the **kB=** capability for the back tab key is not defined in BSD 4.3 *termcap*.

* *The* **ko=** *Capability (obsolete):*
  The **ko=** capability is obsolete in BSD 4.3. It is described here for the benefit of older systems that did not have all the specially defined key capabilities. If your keyboard has other, named function keys (such as a CLEAR key, or a SCROLL key), list these special functions in the **ko=** capability. The format is to list the two-letter capability name, separated by commas, of the equivalent functions. For example, if your terminal has CLEAR and SCROLL, the *termcap* entry would be:

  ```
  ko=cl,sf
  ```

  Even in older systems, the **ko=** capability is rarely used.

EXTENDED SPECIAL KEY DESCRIPTIONS

Terminfo	Termcap	Description
kbeg=	@1=	Describe beginning key.
kcan=	@2=	Describe cancel key.
kclo=	@3=	Describe close key.
kcmd=	@4=	Describe command key.
kcpy=	@5=	Describe copy key.
kcrt=	@6=	Describe create key.
kend=	@7=	Describe end key.
kent=	@8=	Describe enter/send key.
kext=	@9=	Describe exit key.
kfnd=	@0=	Describe find key.
khelp=	%1=	Describe help key.
kmrk=	%2=	Describe mark key.
kmsg=	%3=	Describe message key.
kmov=	%4=	Describe move key.
knxt=	%5=	Describe next-object key.
kopn=	%6=	Describe open key.
kopt=	%7=	Describe options key.
kprv=	%8=	Describe previous-object key.
kprt=	%9=	Describe print or copy key.
krdo=	%0=	Describe redo key.
kref=	&1=	Describe reference key.
krfr=	&2=	Describe refresh key.
krpl=	&3=	Describe replace key.
krst=	&4=	Describe restart key.
kres=	&5=	Describe resume key.
ksav=	&6=	Describe save key.
kspd=	&7=	Describe suspend key.
kund=	&8=	Describe undo key.
kBEG=	&9=	Describe shifted beginning key.
kCAN=	&0=	Describe shifted cancel key.

EXTENDED SPECIAL KEY DESCRIPTIONS (CONT'D)

Terminfo	Termcap	Description
kCMD=	*1=	Describe shifted command key.
kCPY=	*2=	Describe shifted copy key.
kCRT=	*3=	Describe shifted create key.
kDC=	*4=	Describe shifted delete-char key.
kDL=	*5=	Describe shifted delete-line key.
kslt=	*6=	Describe select key.
kEND=	*7=	Describe shifted end key.
kEOL=	*8=	Describe shifted clear-line key.
kEXT=	*9=	Describe shifted exit key.
kFND=	*0=	Describe shifted find key.
kHLP=	#1=	Describe shifted help key.
kHOM=	#2=	Describe shifted home key.
kIC=	#3=	Describe shifted input key.
kLFT=	#4=	Describe shifted left arrow key.
kSAV=	!1=	Describe shifted save key.
kSPD=	!2=	Describe shifted suspend key.
kUND=	!3=	Describe shifted undo key.
kMSG=	%a=	Describe shifted message key.
kMOV=	%b=	Describe shifted move key.
kNXT=	%c=	Describe shifted next key.
kOPT=	%d=	Describe shifted options key.
kPRV=	%e=	Describe shifted prev key.
kPRT=	%f=	Describe shifted print key.
kRDO=	%g=	Describe shifted redo key.
kRPL=	%h=	Describe shifted replace key.
kRIT=	%i=	Describe shifted right arrow key.
kRES=	%j=	Describe shifted resume key.

In addition to the special keys described previously, *terminfo* defines additional special key capabilities. These capabilities are not defined in BSD 4.3 *termcap*, but AT&T has suggested equivalent *termcap* capability names.

NON-STANDARD
CONTROL CHARACTERS

Terminfo	*Termcap*	*Description*
nl=		Newline if not ^J (obsolete).
bc=		Backspace if not ^H (obsolete).

Most terminals use the same standard set of control characters. A new-line is usually sent by ^J, a tab by ^I, and a backspace by ^H. These values will be used by default. In addition, *termcap* assumes that a carriage return is sent by ^M (*terminfo* makes no such assumption). For terminals that do not support these standards, the **nl=**, **bc=**, **cr=** and **ta=** (*hts=* in *terminfo*) capability strings may be set. They allow you to specify non-standard control characters for your terminal. The tab stop capability is discussed in Chapter 10, and the carriage return capability is discussed in Chapter 8.

These capabilities also give you the opportunity to insert padding time with the control character commands. The **nl=** capability in particular may require some padding.

For example, if your terminal needs 10 milliseconds to process a new-line, although using the normal ^J tab character, you can specify:

```
nl=10^J
```

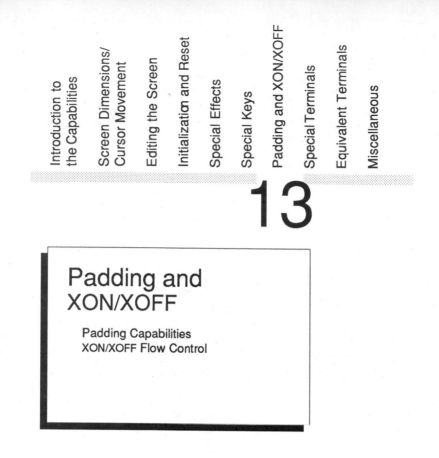

Some terminals are unable to receive a command or a printing character until a certain amount of time has passed. This delay is called padding.

The pad character is a character that does nothing, meant to delay the execution of subsequent commands. Commands are padded by sending the pad character(s) following the command. The number of times the pad character is sent is determined by the length of time the command should be padded and by the baud rate.

Alternatively, a terminal may use the XON/XOFF protocol instead of padding. XON/XOFF is a system in which the terminal may send the XOFF control character (usually ^S) when it needs a pause in the transmission, and the XON control character (usually ^Q) when it is ready to receive again.

Chapter 3 contains a more lengthy description of padding and padding syntax and how padding interrelates with XON/XOFF.

PADDING
CAPABILITIES

Terminfo	Termcap	Description
pad=	pc=	Pad character if not NULL.
npc	NP	No pad character (not in BSD 4.3).
nxon	nx	No padding, must use XON/XOFF (not in BSD 4.3).
rmp=	rP=	Padding after char typed in replace mode (not in BSD 4.3).
pb#	pb#	Padding baud: no padding necessary at baud rate < pb#.

- *Resetting the Pad Character:*
  By default, the pad character is the NULL character (ASCII 000). If a terminal uses anything else, it should be specified in *termcap* in the **pc=** string capability, and in *terminfo* in the *pad=* capability. You should not specify more than one character, since only the first character of the specified string will be used.

- *If There is No Pad Character:*
  In addition, *terminfo* provides for another uncommon case: if the terminal has no pad character, the *npc* Boolean capability should be specified. If the *npc* capability is specified, programs must use the XON/XOFF protocol or stall internally without sending a character to the terminal. The *termcap* equivalent (**NP**) is included in earlier versions of *termcap*, but it is not defined in BSD 4.3 *termcap*.

- *If the Terminal Cannot Use Padding:*
  If the terminal cannot use padding, but must use the XON/XOFF system, use the Boolean capability **nx** in *termcap*, or the *nxon* capability in *terminfo*. This capability and the previous one (*npc* and **NP**) are often used in tandem. See the XON/XOFF section below for a description of that flow control system. **nx** is not defined in BSD 4.3 *termcap*.

- *If Padding is Needed for Characters in Replace Mode:*
  The **rmp=** string capability is a new *terminfo* capability modeled on
  the old *termcap* **ip=** capability (described in Chapter 9). It is used
  to specify padding if padding is needed after characters are typed
  while in replace mode. Replace mode is the usual terminal mode,
  where characters typed replace the old characters on the screen
  under the cursor. This is in contrast to insert mode, where the old
  characters are shifted to make room for the new. In *termcap* systems before BSD 4.3, the equivalent of *rmp=* is rP=.

- *Specifying the Lowest Padding Baud Rate:*
  pb# gives the lowest baud rate at which padding is necessary, in
  both *termcap* and *terminfo*. At baud rates slower than **pb#**, programs do not need to pad. Systems differ on whether the minimum
  padding baud rate applies to all capabilities with padding or just to
  the delays embedded in **cr=**, **sf=** (*ind=*), **le=** (*cub1=*), **ff=** and **ta=**
  (*ht=*), and the obsolete *termcap* parameters **dC=**, **dN=**, **dB=**, **dF=**
  and **dT=**. On most systems, **pb#** applies to all capabilities. In the
  latter case, other, more complicated capabilities may still need padding. Refer to your own system documentation to determine how it
  uses **pb#**.

XON/XOFF
FLOW CONTROL

Terminfo	Termcap	Description
xon	xo	Terminal performs XON/XOFF flow control.
smxon=	SX=	Turn on XON/XOFF flow control (not in BSD 4.3).
rmxon=	RX=	Turn off XON/XOFF flow control (not in BSD 4.3).
xonc=	XN=	XON character: character to turn on input if not ^Q (not in BSD 4.3).
xoffc=	XF=	XOFF character: character to turn off input if not ^S (not in BSD 4.3).

XON/XOFF is a flow control system which is an alternative to padding. Chapter 3 gives a full description of XON/XOFF and padding. XON/XOFF is easier for the program, since UNIX does the work of managing XON/XOFF. In general, *terminfo* programs are run using XON/XOFF instead of padding. *terminfo* also supplies a mechanism for "mandatory padding," which is padding which will be sent even when in XON/XOFF mode. See Chapter 3 for more information.

- *If Your Terminal Uses XON/XOFF:*
  The XON/XOFF capabilities are straightforward once one understands the system. In *termcap*, the Boolean capability **xo** indicates that the terminal uses the XON/XOFF protocol; in *terminfo*, this capability is called *xon*.

  The **nx** *termcap* capability and the *nxon* *terminfo* capability is described in the previous section of this chapter.

  If your terminal uses the XON/XOFF protocol, you should still specify padding information so that programs can compare capabilities to find the most effective way to handle an overflow situation. See Chapter 3 for more information.

- *Enabling and Disabling XON/XOFF (not in BSD 4.3):*
  If the terminal uses special strings to switch in and out of
  XON/XOFF mode, these strings need to be specified. The string to
  go into XON/XOFF mode should be kept in the **SX=** capability in
  termcap and in the ***smxon=*** capability in *terminfo*. The string to
  leave XON/XOFF mode should be kept in the **RX=** capability in
  termcap and in the ***rmxon=*** capability in *terminfo*.

- *Specifying the XON and XOFF Characters:*
  If the terminal uses characters besides ^Q and ^S for the
  XON/XOFF characters, specify these special characters in **XN=** and
  XF= in *termcap*, and in ***xonc=*** and ***xoffc=*** in *terminfo*.

xo is the only XON/XOFF capability defined for *termcap* in BSD 4.3.
xonc= and *xonc=* are primarily used by *terminfo*, and possibly by
future implementations of *termcap*.

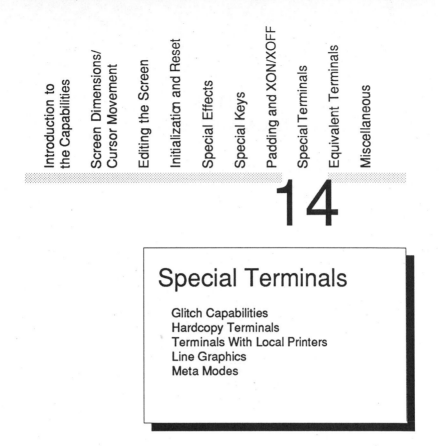

Introduction to the Capabilities

Screen Dimensions/ Cursor Movement

Editing the Screen

Initialization and Reset

Special Effects

Special Keys

Padding and XON/XOFF

Special Terminals

Equivalent Terminals

Miscellaneous

14

Special Terminals

Glitch Capabilities
Hardcopy Terminals
Terminals With Local Printers
Line Graphics
Meta Modes

This chapter covers "special" features which your terminal may have. Included in this chapter are capabilities relating to hardcopy (paper) terminals, terminals with local printers, terminals with a line-drawing alternate character set, and terminals with a meta key.

Also covered in this chapter are what we call "glitches." Glitches are features which conflict with the way other terminals normally work, and hence with the way a program might expect it to work. They are peculiarities which may cause trouble if the program is not kept aware of it. You should become familiar with the list of glitches, because it just might turn up that your terminal has one of them.

GLITCH
CAPABILITIES

Terminfo	Termcap	Description
xenl	xn	Newline or wraparound glitch.
xsb	xb	Beehive glitch. (F1 key sends ESCAPE, F2 key sends ^C.)
	xr	Return glitch: return character clears the line (obsolete).
xhp	xs	Standout glitch: text typed over standout text is automatically in standout mode.
xt	xt	Teleray glitch: has destructive tabs and odd standout mode.
hz	hz	Hazeltine glitch: cannot print tildes (~).
	xx	Tektronix 4025 line insert problem (obsolete).
	nc	No correctly working carriage return glitch (obsolete).
	ns	Abnormal scroll even though terminal is CRT (obsolete).

A "glitch" is what *termcap* developers call a peculiarity a terminal may have that is inconsistent with most other terminals, and hence inconsistent with the intended effects of many programs.

Most of the glitch capabilities begin with the letter "x" in honor of Xanthippe. Xanthippe was Socrates' wife, whom history records as nagging and unpleasant. Xanthippe capabilities are Boolean capabilities of a similar rude nature.

- *The Newline Glitch:*
  Of all the glitches recorded here, the newline glitch is the only one that is fairly common. This glitch means that the terminal does not wrap from the rightmost column in the expected way. If your

terminal has this glitch, specify the **xn** capability in *termcap* or the *xenl* capability in *terminfo*.

There are two sorts of newline glitch specified by this glitch. The first type occurs on terminals like the Concept-100, in which wraparound is suppressed if the character causing the wraparound is a newline. Otherwise, the terminal performs normal automargins. To test whether your terminal has this type of glitch, create a file with exactly 80 printing characters on each line (plus the newline), and *cat* the file to the screen. If the file comes out single spaced, your terminal is suppressing wraparound on the newline, and so should have **xn** in its database entry.

The second type occurs on DEC vt100 terminals using automatic margins. They wrap only when the character is a graphics (printing) character, suppressing wrapping for all control characters. Programs must be careful when using terminals with the newline glitch, because normal assumptions about cursor positioning may not be true. The safest way is to use absolute cursor motion to place the cursor in a known position after writing a non-graphic character in the last column.

- *The Beehive Superbee Glitch:*
  Some Beehive Superbee terminals were unable to transmit $\boxed{\text{ESCAPE}}$ or ^C. Only certain Superbees had this problem, depending on their ROMs. The glitch created for those terminals is called **xb** in *termcap*, and *xsb* in *terminfo*. It tells programs to pretend that the F1 key sends $\boxed{\text{ESCAPE}}$, and F2 sends ^C. Such terminals are rare, and so this glitch is of more concern to Superbee owners than programmers.

- *The Carriage Return Glitch:*
  When a carriage return is entered in the middle of a line of text, the cursor should simply go to the beginning of the current line. Some terminals, however, have the peculiarity that they will clear to the end of that line before going to the beginning of the next line, and the glitch created for those terminals is called **xr** in *termcap*, the return glitch. This capability is considered obsolete in *terminfo* because *cr=* should always be specified if the carriage return acts as it is supposed to.

- *The Standout Glitch:*
  While your terminal is in standout mode, the text typed should also be in standout mode. Terminals which do not do this should use the standout glitch, which is **xs** in *termcap* and *xhp* in *terminfo*.

  If the terminal uses magic cookies to start standout mode, the way to change that region of the screen back from standout mode to normal mode is to delete the part of the line that includes the magic cookie. If the terminal uses a mark with each character to indicate that that character should be in standout mode, then the way to change it back to normal mode is by clearing that part of the line with the most appropriate clear capability. See Chapter 11 for more information.

- *The Teleray Glitch:*
  The **xt** capability (in both *termcap* and *terminfo*) is meant to compensate for the Teleray terminal, which has two glitches, covering two idiosyncrasies: destructive tabs and a peculiarity with standout magic cookies.

  a. *Destructive tabs:* Tabs should move the cursor to the next tab stop without changing the underlying text. Destructive tabs are tabs which replace the characters that were at those locations with spaces. Terminals with this feature are largely obsolete. The **xt** capability is designed to compensate for this glitch.

  b. *Standout magic cookies:* The **xt** glitch also means that to change a region displayed in standout mode back to normal mode, you cannot just type over the standout text but have to use one of two alternate methods: either delete the line with the standout text on it or position the cursor before the start of the standout region and use the "standout end" string.

- *The Hazeltine (Tilde) Glitch:*
  Terminals which do not have a tilde ("~") are covered by the Hazeltine glitch **hz** in both *termcap* and *terminfo*. Hazeltine terminals use a tilde in escape command sequences for cursor motion and the like, making this character unavailable for general use. Programs must not send tildes to these terminals or else they can have amazing, unpredictable effects on the screen. All tildes must be deleted or replaced with something innocuous in output to such terminals. Since such terminals are becoming increasingly rare, handling **hz** terminals properly should be a relatively low

priority for programmers. It is more important for users of such terminals to know what could be causing strange behavior.

- *The Line Insert Glitch (obsolete):*
The Tektronix 4025 terminal has a line insert problem, which is covered by the **xx** capability. It is an obsolete capability that is not implemented in *terminfo*.

- *The No Carriage Return Glitch (obsolete):*
A carriage return should move the cursor to the leftmost column. The **nc** capability should be specified if carriage return has any other effects, such as performing an automatic newline, or if there is no carriage return at all.

Terminals will often seem to do a newline automatically on a carriage return, because the system is echoing a carriage return and a newline together. This automatic newline is not a glitch, it is the desired result of the system sending two characters. The **nc** glitch is set only if the terminal, not the system, is adding a newline.

Programs can work around the **nc** glitch by using cursor movement to go to the start of a line. This glitch is rare, so assume your terminal does have a return unless you are forced to believe that it does not. This capability is officially obsolete in *terminfo* but is equivalent to not specifying *cr=* in the entry.

- *Abnormal Scrolling (obsolete):*
On most modern terminals, sending a newline while the cursor is on the bottom line of the screen causes the terminal to scroll up one line. If you have an older terminal, scrolling may not work this way, in which case you should specify the **ns** capability. Note that some terminals can have an explicit scroll command but still not scroll properly and may require you to specify both **ns** and the scroll forward command (**sf=** in *termcap*, or *ind=* in *terminfo*).

HARDCOPY TERMINALS

Terminfo	Termcap	Description
hc	hc	Terminal is a hardcopy terminal.
	dB#	Delay (in milliseconds) for back-space on hardcopy terminal (obsolete).
	dC#	Delay (in milliseconds) for carriage return on hardcopy terminal (obsolete).
	dF#	Delay (in milliseconds) for formfeed on hardcopy terminal (obsolete).
	dN#	Delay (in milliseconds) for newline on hardcopy terminal (obsolete).
	dT#	Delay (in milliseconds) for tab on hardcopy terminal (obsolete).
	dV#	Delay (in milliseconds) for vertical tab on hardcopy terminal (obsolete).
ff=	ff=	Formfeed character on hardcopy terminals if not ^L.

The hardcopy capabilities are defined only for hardcopy terminals, and as a result, they are seldom used. Programs need to know that a hardcopy terminal is being used, so that they can modify their output to work around the unavoidable limitations. *vi*, for example, can work on a limited open mode on hardcopy terminals but needs to know to do that first.

- *Specifying a Hardcopy Terminal:*
  The Boolean capability **hc** indicates that the terminal is a hardcopy terminal in both *terminfo* and *termcap*.

- *Delay Capabilities (obsolete):*
  The delay capabilities are numeric capabilities defined primarily for hardcopy terminals. They specify a delay (or padding) which the system should wait after sending the respective character. For example, **dC#20** instructs the system to wait 20 milliseconds after

issuing a carriage return. The default value in all cases is no delay. Hardcopy terminals are more likely to require a delay because of the mechanics of moving paper. The delays are used by *tset* for setting the terminal driver modes. These capabilities are used in BSD 4.2 but are considered obsolete for BSD 4.3, and are unimplemented in *terminfo*. Instead, in BSD 4.3, *tset* takes the delay information from the padding information in cr=, sf=, le=, ff=, and ta=. In System V, the equivalent padding information is set by *tput init*.

- *Formfeed Character:*
  The formfeed character is usually assumed to be ^L. If your hardcopy terminal has a different formfeed character, you need to specify it with the ff= capability (both *termcap* and *terminfo*). The ff= capability is like the other default redefine keys (nl=, ta=, bc=, cr=, and pc=), except it is limited to hardcopy terminals and does not allow for padding. In *termcap*, you can use dF# to specify a padding delay for formfeed.

  At low baud rates, it may not be necessary to pad at all. See the pb# capability in Chapter 13, which gives the lowest baud rate at which padding is necessary.

Related Capabilities For Hardcopy Terminals

Several other capabilities are predominantly, but not exclusively, for hardcopy terminals. The os capability designates terminals which can overstrike one letter on top of another. hu= and hd= are the halfline up and halfline down capabilities, respectively. The os capability is described in Chapter 16 and the halfline capabilities are described in Chapter 8 under "Miscellaneous Local Movements."

TERMINALS WITH LOCAL PRINTERS

Terminfo	Termcap	Description
mc0=	ps=	Print screen contents on auxiliary printer.
mc5=	po=	Turn the printer on
mc4=	pf=	Turn the printer off
mc5p=	pO=	Turn the printer on for #1 bytes (#1 < 256).
mc5i	5i	Printer will not echo on the screen (not in BSD 4.3).

Some terminals (most notably some Hewlett-Packard terminals) have attached auxiliary printers, and many others have printer ports. These printers are local to the terminal and have no relation to the UNIX system printer. This section provides the capabilities to control the printer for such terminals.

- *Turning the Printer On and Off:*
  To turn the printer on, you need to use the **po=** capability in *termcap*, or the *mc4=* capability in *terminfo*. The **ps=** capability in *termcap*, and the *mc0=* capability in *terminfo*, causes the contents of the screen to be printed. All characters sent to the terminal will henceforth be redirected to the printer. To turn the printer off, you can use the **pf=** capability in *termcap*, or the *mc4=* capability in *terminfo*.

- *Turning the Printer On (Parameterized):*
  To turn the printer on for a specified number of bytes, you can use the parameterized **pO=** capability in *termcap*, or the *mc5p=* capability in *terminfo*. The parameter should be less than 256. When the printer is turned on with **pO=**, all text (including the **pf=** printer off sequences) is sent to the printer until the specified number of bytes has been sent. In this way, you can print a **pf=** sequence. This is the best way to send bitmaps or object code files that might inadvertently contain the printer off sequence.

- *Silent Printer (not in BSD 4.3):*
  terminfo has one additional capability that is absent from BSD 4.3
  termcap. The Boolean capability *mc5i* in *terminfo* (and **5i** in older
  version of *termcap*) indicates that the terminal has a silent printer:
  text sent to the printer is not displayed on the terminal screen. In
  termcap systems without **5i**, there is no way to indicate whether the
  printer is silent or noisy, so programs must consider the text sent to
  the screen while printing as undefined.

LINE GRAPHICS

Terminfo	Termcap	Description
acsc=	**ac=**	Map line drawing character set to ASCII characters (not in BSD 4.3).

Some terminals have an alternate character set for line drawing. This character set contains glyphs like an arrow pointing up, bullets, lower left corners, etc. However, there is not an industry standard to map the alternate character set to ordinary ASCII characters. Since there is no such standard, *terminfo* describes the mapping in the string capability *acsc=* instead. In *termcap*, the equivalent is **ac=**, but it is not defined in BSD 4.3.

The capabilities to enable, start and end the alternate character sets are described in Chapter 11.

The *acsc=* capability is based on the alternate character set glyph mapping used by the DEC vt100+, with extensions from the AT&T 4410v1 terminal.

Glyph name	vt100+ Char	Glyph name	vt100+ Char
arrow pointing right	+	*upper left corner*	l
arrow pointing left	,	*lower left corner*	m
arrow pointing down	.	*plus*	n
solid square block	0	*scan line 1*	o
lantern symbol	I	*horizontal line*	q
arrow pointing up	–	*scan line 9*	s
diamond	'	*left tee (⊢)*	t
checker board (stipple)	a	*right tee (⊣)*	u
degree symbol	f	*bottom tee (⊥)*	v
plus/minus	g	*top tee (⊤)*	w
board of squares	h	*vertical line*	x
lower right corner	j	*bullet*	~
upper right corner	k		

Example of Mapping an Alternate Character Set

The following example of mapping alternate character sets is from the AT&T System V documentation.

The best way to define the line drawing character set capability for a new terminal is:

1. Start with the table of the vt100+ graphics characters.
2. Add a third column to that table for the characters sent by the terminal you wish to describe.
3. Go through that terminal's manual, and write in the character that it uses for each glyph in the third column. This will result in a table as shown:

Glyph Name	vt100+ char	New tty char
upper left corner	l	R
lower left corner	m	F
upper right corner	k	T
lower right corner	j	G
horizontal line	q	,
vertical line	x	.

4. Now write down the characters left to right alternating between the vt100+ terminal and the new terminal. For example:

```
acsc=lRmFkTjGq\,x
```

For the vt100 itself, the capability is each character twice.

```
acsc=``aaffggjjkkllmmnnoo ...
```

META MODES

Terminfo	Termcap	Description
km	km	Terminal has a "meta" key.
smm=	mm=	Meta mode on: put terminal into meta mode.
rmm=	mo=	Meta mode off: take terminal out of meta mode.

A meta key is a key which, like the shift key, is pressed with another key to modify the character sent. The effect of the meta key is to set the eighth bit of the character, also called the 0200 bit (octal). In the U.S. market, the eighth bit is usually used as a parity bit and may be stripped by programs. (In the international market, all eight bits are commonly used.)

- *If the Terminal has a Meta Mode:*
  Specifying *km* in both *terminfo* and *termcap* lets programs know that the eighth bit can carry information. It should only be specified for terminals with meta keys.

- *Turning Meta Mode On and Off:*
  If the terminal has string commands to turn meta mode on and off, specify these commands in the *smm=* and *rmm=* capabilities in *terminfo*. The *termcap* equivalent for these are **mm=** and **mo=**, respectively. If a terminal has meta keys that can not be turned off and on, do not use these capabilities.

Introduction to
the Capabilities

Screen Dimensions/
Cursor Movement

Editing the Screen

Initialization and Reset

Special Effects

Special Keys

Padding and XON/XOFF

Special Terminals

Equivalent Terminals

Miscellaneous

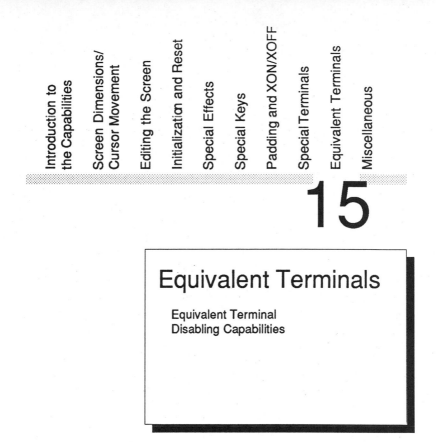

15

Equivalent Terminals

Equivalent Terminal
Disabling Capabilities

Terminal equivalents are a very powerful tool in making a *termcap* or *terminfo* entry more efficient. Using equivalent terminals, the capabilities from one entry can be read into another, and then modified to conform to the peculiarities of the second terminal.

Chapter 5 gives some discussion of the advantages of using equivalent terminals, in the section "Modifying an Entry."

EQUIVALENT TERMINAL

Terminfo	Termcap	Description
use=	tc=	Terminal copy: read terminal capabilities from a similar terminal.

"Terminal copy" is not really a capability, but a command for *terminfo* or *termcap*. It says to transfer the capabilities from another terminal entry in the database into the current one, thus making the terminals equivalent. It can be used to make the entry more efficient, not only by reducing redundancies but also by ensuring that related entries are kept consistent.

If included, the **tc=** (*termcap*) or **use=** request should be the last field in the entry. Capabilities that have already been defined in the current entry will be ignored when the equivalent terminal entry is copied.

termcap and *terminfo* treat equivalent terminals differently. *terminfo* allows more than one **use=** capability to be given, while BSD 4.3 *termcap* specifies that **tc=** must be last field in the entry, thus implying that more than one **tc=** capability may not be used. BSD 4.3 *termcap* also restricts the total size of the combined entries to 1024, while *terminfo* makes no size restriction.

In *termcap*, a terminal entry should precede any other entries which reference it with a **tc=** request. You may create a chain of **tc=** capabilities, as long as it is not recursive or too long. ("Too long" is determined by the system, which will print the error message "Infinite tc= loop" when it tries to use *termcap* for that terminal.)

Disabling Capabilities

There are cases in which you want to use most, but not all, of the capabilities in another terminal description. Specifying an "@" in a capability definition indicates that the current terminal does not have that capability, even though the terminal specified through tc= or *use=* does.

The canceled capability must precede the capability which reads from another entry. For example, if there was a terminal which does everything the Wyse-50 does except it cannot do automargins, its capabilities could be defined as:

```
:am@:tc=wy50:        (termcap)

am@,  use=wy50,      (terminfo)
```

Examples

Suppose you have a complete entry for the DEC vt100, and you would like to include an entry for the vt100 in 132-column mode. The *termcap* entry for the 132-column vt100 can be simply:

```
dt|vt100-w|dec vt100 132 columns (w/ advanced video):\
    :co#132:tc=vt100:
```

In *terminfo*, this might read:

```
vt100-w|dec vt100 132 columns (w/ advanced video),
    cols#132, use=vt100,
```

After setting the columns to 132, this entry then reads in all the information for a vt100. Since the number of columns is already set, the co#80 or *cols#80* capability of the vt100 is ignored.

If you were setting your 132-column vt100 so that it would also not have automatic margins, the *termcap* entry could be:

```
du|vt100-w-nam|vt100-nam-w|dec vt100 132 cols, no am:\
    :co#132:am@:tc=vt100:
```

Or in *terminfo*:

```
vt100-w-nam|vt100-nam-w|dec vt100 132 cols, no am,
    cols#132, am@, use=vt100,
```

The Boolean **am** capability is blocked by the "@". You can keep string capabilities from being set in just the same way, by following their two-letter abbreviation with an "@". For example, **ho@** (in *termcap*) or *home@* (in *terminfo*) would keep the home capability string from being set by a later **ho=** or *homes=* specification in an equivalenced entry.

Introduction to
the Capabilities

Screen Dimensions/
Cursor Movement

Editing the Screen

Initialization and Reset

Special Effects

Special Keys

Padding and XON/XOFF

Special Terminals

Equivalent Terminals

Miscellaneous

16

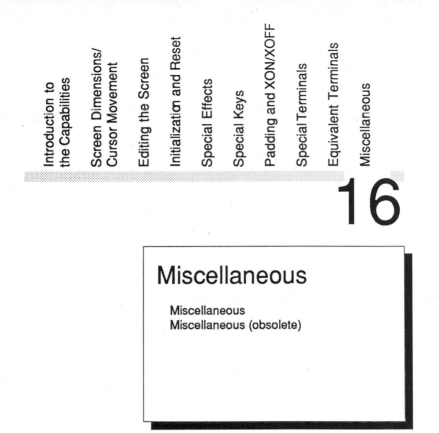

Miscellaneous

Miscellaneous
Miscellaneous (obsolete)

As you would expect from a chapter titled "Miscellaneous," this chapter includes all the odds and ends which did not fit in any of the previous chapters.

There are actually two types of "miscellaneous" capabilities covered in this chapter: those which are obsolete, and those which are not. The obsolete capabilities are not very important, so they are listed last.

MISCELLANEOUS

Terminfo	Termcap	Description
am	**am**	Terminal does automargin (wrap-around).
os	**os**	Terminal can overstrike without erasing character.
bw	**bw**	Backwards wrap, backspacing off left edge. Wraps cursor to right edge, previous line.
eo	**eo**	A space erases all characters at cursor even though terminal over-strikes.
lm#	**lm#**	Lines of Memory: explicit 0 means varies.
gn	**gn**	Generic terminal descriptions for dialup, switch, patch, network, etc.
vt#	**vt#**	Virtual terminal number (not supported on all BSD 4.3 systems).
rfi=	**RF=**	Request for input: system ready for next input character (not in BSD 4.3).
wind=	**wi=**	Current window is lines #1 through #2, columns #3 through #4 (mainly terminfo).
cmdch=	**CC=**	Command character: dummy command character in string commands, replaced at run time with CC environment variable.

The automatic margin capability in this section is quite common. Most of the other capabilities are seldom used.

- *Automatic Right Margin (Wraparound):*
  Most terminals have the property of automatically wrapping to the start of the next line when a line goes off the right edge of the screen. This is called an automatic margin and is specified in both *termcap* and *terminfo* by the Boolean capability **am**.

If you are not sure if your terminal has this feature, you can check directly on the terminal by typing a long line.

Some terminals (notably the Concept-100 and the vt100) perform automatic margins most of the time, but suppress wrapping for certain characters. For these terminals, you should specify both the **am** and **xn** capabilities. See the **xn** capability in Chapter 14 for more information about these terminals.

- *Overstrike:*
  Overstrike means that when a character is typed in at the position of an existing character, the original character is not overwritten but remains on the screen, creating a compound character. This feature is specified in both *termcap* and *terminfo* by the Boolean **os** capability.

  It should be fairly simple to test for this capability on your terminal. In general, hardcopy terminals have the **os** capability (for obvious reasons) and video terminals do not. Some video terminals, notably the Tektronic 4010, use a storage scope and thus do have the overstrike capability. APL terminals and some bitmap terminals can overstrike too.

- *Backward Wrapping:*
  bw is the Boolean backspace wrap capability in both *terminfo* and *termcap*. A terminal with backwards wrapping is one that moves the cursor to the end of the previous line if you backspace while it is at the beginning of a line.

- *If Overstriking Terminal can Erase with a Space:*
  eo is specified for overstriking terminals that allow a space placed on top of a character to erase the character. This is the way that most terminals erase. However, most overstriking terminals (which will have the **os** capability) are hardcopy terminals, and typing a space on top of a character will certainly not remove the ink from the paper. **eo** is a capability for those rare video terminals that overstrike and erase a character by typing a space on top (see the **os** overstrike capability).

- *If the Terminal has Extra Screen Memory:*
  Some terminals have more lines of memory dedicated to the screen than can be displayed simultaneously. If there is a fixed number of lines of memory available, that number should be specified with the **lm#** capability. It should be set to the **total** number of lines of

memory dedicated to the display, not just the additional lines not shown on the screen. If the number of lines is variable (i.e., depends on the number of characters per line), then **lm#** should be explicitly set to zero. If the terminal does not have extra memory for the screen, you can omit this capability or set it equal to the total number of lines on the screen.

- *Generic Terminal Descriptions:*
  It is useful to include generic terminal descriptions such as switch, dialup, patch and network in the *termcap* and *terminfo* databases. These entries should contain the most basic capabilities compatible with most any terminal accessing the system in that way. The purpose of a generic description is so that the terminal can limp along until the user specifies the real terminal type. Such generic descriptions must be very bland—too bland to do anything demanding with.

  Generic terminal entries in both *terminfo* and *termcap* should contain the **gn** capability, so that programs know that they are working with a generic entry and can complain that having a bland entry makes some operations impossible. Those programs can then ask the user for their real terminal type. (In contrast, if the user simply has a weak terminal instead of a generic terminal, the program knows that the problem is inherent to the terminal, not the description.)

  There is an example of a generic entry in Chapter 2 of this book.

  The **gn** capability does not apply if the terminal is supported through the UNIX system *virtual* protocol. See the description of the vt# capability below.

- *Virtual Terminals:*
  vt# gives the virtual terminal number if the terminal is one of those supported by the UNIX system virtual terminal protocol. (Virtual terminals are a method for allowing programs to access a single physical screen as if it were several distinct terminals.)

- *Line Turn Around Sequence (not in BSD 4.3):*
  rfi= is another capability created for *terminfo*. Its nominal *termcap* equivalent is **RF=**, but it is not available in BSD 4.3 *termcap*. It specifies a line turn around sequence, that is, a sequence which should be transmitted by the system between sending and receiving characters. This is mostly used with special communication links, such as that used by virtual terminals communicating across a pipe.

- *Defining a Window on the Screen (mainly terminfo):*
  Some terminals (not many) can define a window as part of memory which all clearing, deletion, insertion, scrolling and wrapping commands will affect. The *terminfo* capability for creating such a window is the **wind=** capability, and the *termcap* equivalence is **wi=**. The capability takes four parameters: the starting line, the end line, the start column, and the end column—in that order. The **wi=** *termcap* equivalent is defined primarily for compatibility, since most *termcap* systems will not be able to use it.

- *Settable Control Character:*
  The control character is the first character in commands that control the terminal and, thus, is also the first character in string capabilities. It lets the terminal know that the following string is a control string. Generally, the command character appears literally as the first character of a string capability. Although some terminals use only one control character, some others use several different ones, and some terminals (like the Tektronix 4025) allow the control character to be set to one of a number of characters.

  Some terminals allow the control character to be reset, and for those terminals, a mechanism has been devised to redefine it without having to rewrite the entire entry, using an environment variable which may be set on the command line or within a program. The *cmdch=* capability in *terminfo*, and the **CC=** capability in *termcap*, has been designed to carry a "dummy" control character. This dummy character will be written as the first character of the string capabilities which need a control character. The actual control character to be substituted will be kept in the CC environment variable, which may be redefined by programs at run time.

  When a command is to be issued, programs will read the string capability, replace the dummy command character of the **CC=** capability with the real command character from the CC environment variable, and then send the correct command to the terminal.

  Part of one *termcap* entry for the Tektronix 4025 looks like:

  ```
  :CC=^_:al=^_up\r^_ili:cd=^_dli 50\r:ta=^I:
  ```

  This entry would define the dummy command character as ^_ and replace ^_ at run time with the character in the CC environment variable. Note that the command character can appear more than once in a string, or it can be omitted altogether if unnecessary.

Not all UNIX systems support the this mechanism, and it can cause conflicts with the *make* program. Furthermore, there are few terminals which have resettable command characters. As a result, this capability is rarely used.

MISCELLANEOUS
(OBSOLETE)

Termcap	Description
EP	Even Parity (obsolete).
OP	Odd Parity (obsolete).
HD	Half Duplex (obsolete).
LC	Lower Case (obsolete).
UC	Upper Case (obsolete).
NL	\n is a newline, not a linefeed (obsolete).
ml=	Memory lock: turn memory lock on above cursor (obsolete).
mu=	Memory unlock: turn off memory lock above cursor (obsolete).

The capabilities in this section are not defined in *terminfo* and are consequently considered obsolete by BSD 4.3 *termcap*. In fact, these capabilities are also missing from some *termcap* systems older than BSD 4.3 as well. In general, they are unnecessary and should be avoided. They are documented here only to make our discussion of the *termcap* capabilities complete.

The first five capabilities are self-explanatory, simply describing some limitations which plagued some older terminals. **NL** is for terminals which do a linefeed and carriage return when given the \n character, instead of just a linefeed.

- *Memory Locks:*
  Some terminals, like the Hewlett-Packard 2645, have a memory lock, which protects the screen memory above the cursor from changes. This is usually seen on multi-page terminals. The **ml=** capability turns that lock on, **mu=** turns it off. These capabilities are not included on all systems.

Part 3: Appendices

There are four appendices included.

Appendix A, *Capabilities Used by vi*, gives a full listing of the capabilities which the *vi* screen editor uses.

Appendix B, *Accessing Termcap From a C Program*, is a description of the routines provided by the Termcap Library and the Terminfo Library's emulation of *termcap*.

Appendix C, *Accessing Terminfo From a C Program*, describes the routines provided by for *terminfo* in the Curses Library. It also lists the C variable names for the *terminfo* capabilities.

Appendix D, *List of Capabilities*, is an alphabetical listing of all the capabilities covered in Chapters 8 through 16, with *termcap* and *terminfo* intermixed.

A

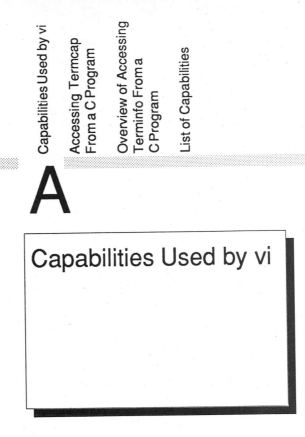

Capabilities Used by vi

vi is a program built on the capabilities described in the *termcap* database. Thus, if a *termcap* entry does not supply these capabilities, *vi* may not work properly, if at all. Below is a list of the capabilities used by *vi*. Just because *vi* looks for a capability does not mean that you have to have it defined in your entry. It is fairly obvious which ones are essential for performing the kinds of screen updating functions that are necessary in *vi*.

Although *terminfo* equivalences are listed here, beware that this list was taken from the *termcap* version of *vi*, not from the *terminfo* version.

Termcap	Terminfo	Description
al	*il1*	Add new blank line.
AL	*il*	Add *n* blank lines.
am	*am*	Terminal has automatic margins.
bc	*None*	Backspace if not ^H.
bs	*None*	Terminal can backspace with ^H.
bt	*cbt*	Back tab.
cd	*ed*	Clear to end of display.
ce	*el*	Clear to end of line.
cl	*clear*	Clear screen.
cm	*cup*	Cursor motion.
cr	*cr*	Carriage return (default ^M).
cs	*csr*	Change scrolling region (vt100).
da	*da*	Display may be retained above.
db	*db*	Display may be retained below.
dc	*dch1*	Delete character.
dl	*dl1*	Delete line.
DL	*dl*	Delete *n* lines.
dm	*smdc*	Delete mode (enter).
do	*cud1*	Down one line.
DO	*cud*	Move cursor down *n* lines.
ed	*rmdc*	End delete mode.
ei	*rmir*	End insert mode; give ":ei=:" if **ic**.
eo	*eo*	Can erase overstrikes with a blank.
hc	*hc*	Hardcopy terminal.
ho	*home*	Home cursor (if no **cm**).
hz	*hz*	Hazeltine; cannot print tildes ("~").
ic	*ich1*	Insert character.
im	*smir*	Insert mode (enter); give ":im=:" if **ic**.
in	*in*	Insert mode distinguishes nulls on display.
ip	*ip*	Insert pad after character inserted.
k0-k9	*kf0-kf9*	Sent by "other" function keys 0 through 9.
kd	*kcud1*	Sent by terminal down arrow key.
ke	*rmkx*	Out of "keypad transmit" mode.
kh	*khome*	Sent by home key.
kl	*kcub1*	Sent by terminal left arrow key.
kr	*kcuf1*	Sent by terminal right arrow key.
ks	*smkx*	Put terminal in "keypad transmit" mode.
ku	*kcuu1*	Sent by terminal up arrow key.
LE	*cub*	Move cursor left *n* spaces.
ll	*ll*	Last line, first column (if no **cm**).
mi	*mir*	Safe to move while in insert mode.

Termcap	Terminfo	Description
nc	*None*	No correctly working carriage return (DM2500, H2000).
nd	*cuf1*	Non-destructive space (cursor right).
nl	*None*	Newline character (default 0.
ns	*None*	Terminal is a CRT but does not scroll.
os	*os*	Terminal overstrikes.
pc	*pad*	Pad character (rather than null).
RI	*cuf*	Move cursor right *n* spaces.
se	*rmso*	End standout mode.
sf	*ind*	Scroll forwards.
so	*smso*	Begin standout mode.
sr	*ri*	Scroll reverse (backwards).
ta	*ht*	Tab (other than ^I or with padding).
te	*rmcup*	String to end programs that use **cm**.
ti	*smcup*	String to begin programs that use **cm**.
ul	*ul*	Terminal underlines even though it does not overstrike.
up	*cuu1*	Upline (cursor up).
UP	*cuu*	Move cursor up *n* lines.
vb	*flash*	Visible bell (may not move cursor).
ve	*cnorm*	Sequence to end open/visual mode (undo vi/vs).
vs	*cvvis*	Sequence to start open/visual mode.
xb	*xsb*	Beehive (f1=escape, f2=ctrl C).
xn	*xenl*	A newline is ignored after a wrap (Concept).
xt	*xt*	Tabs are destructive, magic **so** character (Teleray 1061).

Special thanks to Phil Hill of Vmark Software, Inc. for compiling this information and making it available to us.

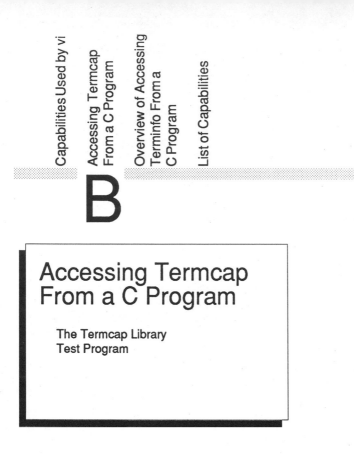

Capabilities Used by vi

Accessing Termcap From a C Program

Overview of Accessing Terminfo From a C Program

List of Capabilities

B

Accessing Termcap From a C Program

The Termcap Library
Test Program

This appendix is intended for C programmers and will only make sense if you know the C programming language.

There are two ways to access the *termcap* data base from within your programs: through *curses* or through *termlib*.

- *curses*

    The *curses* library contains a complete set of routines for managing a screen display. *curses* routines use information extracted from the *termcap* database and provide a convenient interface to the programmer. The *curses* routines attempt to optimize terminal output by determining the most efficient methods for moving the cursor or updating the display. They also are clever enough to seek alternate methods for an operation if a particular capability does not exist.

196

curses routines are recommended as a general purpose interface to *termcap*, since they free the programmer from the nitty gritty details of the terminal database. *curses* is described in the Nutshell Handbook *Programming with Curses* and in the reference pages of your system documentation.

*   **termlib**

    If you find that *curses* routines are too large or otherwise inappropriate to your task, or if you simply wish to experience the exhilaration of accomplishing a simple task in a difficult way, then use the *termlib* library. *termlib* contains routines to provide low-level access to the *termcap* database—the same routines, in fact, which *curses* uses to extract *termcap* capability information. By calling these routines through your own program, you gain direct access to the database at the expense of additional programming complexity.

The Termcap Library

To use the *termcap* routines, you must compile with the *-ltermlib* option. (On some systems, the library is linked with *-ltermcap* instead.) On *terminfo* systems, these functions are present in *-lcurses*. The library routines are as follows.

Function and Arguments	Description
`char *getenv(var)` `char *var`	Get value of environment variable `var`.
`int tgetent(bp, name)` `char *bp, *name`	Read entry for terminal type `name` into buffer `bp`.
`int tgetflag(cap)` `char *cap`	Return value of Boolean capability `cap`.
`int tgetnum(cap)` `char *cap`	Return value of Boolean capability `cap`.
`char *tgetstr(cap, buf)` `char *cap, **buf`	Return pointer to string capability `cap` copied into `buf`.

`char *tgoto(cm,col,lin)`	Return string to move cursor
`char *cm;`	to `(col,lin)`.
`int   col, line;`	
`tputs(cp, affcnt, outc)`	Decodes and pads capability
`char *cp;`	string to output lines
`int affcnt, (*outc)( );`	affected and output function.

External Variables	Description
`extern char PC;`	Pad character.
`extern char *BC;`	Backspace string.
`extern char *UP`	Cursor up string.
`extern short ospeed;`	Output speed.

Declarations for the above functions and variables should appear at the beginning of any program that uses them.

getenv returns a pointer to a string which contains the value of an environment variable. In the context of *termlib* programming, it is called with the argument "TERM" to determine the name of your terminal type and returns a pointer to a string such as "vt100". This pointer must be saved and used as the `name` argument to a subsequent tgetent call. getenv is actually found in the standard C library, not in *termlib*, but it is described here since it is so frequently used with the *termlib* library.

The tgetent routine locates and loads the complete *termcap* entry for your terminal. It is passed a buffer address *bp*, to which the entry is copied, and the `name` of your terminal type, usually taken from a previous getenv call. The buffer must be 1024 bytes in size and must be retained while you call tgetflag, tgetnum, and tgetstr to find out individual capability values. tgetent returns −1 if it could not open the *termcap* file, 0 if the terminal name is not found, and 1 if successful.

tgetent normally looks in the system default *termcap* file */etc/termcap*. This choice can be overridden through the environment variable TERMCAP, which is most commonly set in your shell's login initialization file. If set, TERMCAP must contain either the name of an alternate *termcap* file or the *termcap* entry itself. The TERMCAP variable is useful for both debugging new entries or simply adding a new entry when you have no permission to modify the */etc/termcap* file. It is also useful in speeding up the loading of the *termcap* entry, since it can eliminate the scanning of a large */etc/termcap* file.

If TERMCAP is set in the environment, `tgetent` uses the following rules to interpret it. First, if the TERMCAP string begins with a slash, then it is assumed to be the pathname of a file to be read instead of the */etc/termcap* file. Otherwise, if TERMCAP does not begin with a slash, and if the *name* argument passed to `tgetent` matches the "TERM" environment variable, then TERMCAP is interpreted as the *termcap* entry itself. If *name* does not match "TERM" and TERMCAP is not a pathname, then TERMCAP is ignored.

Once the *termcap* entry is loaded with `tgetent`, individual capability values may be extracted with the routines `tgetflag`, `tgetnum`, and `tgetstr`. All three routines look for entries in the same buffer which was passed to `tgetent`; the buffer address is saved by `tgetent` and need not be passed as an argument to the `tgetflag`, `tgetnum`, and `tgetstr`.

`tgetflag` determines the value of a Boolean capability *cap*. *cap* should be the two-letter name of the *termcap* capability, such as **am** (automatic margins). If the Boolean capability is present in the entry, `tgetflag` returns 1, otherwise it is absent and `tgetflag` returns 0.

`tgetnum` operates like `tgetflag` but is passed the name of a numeric *termcap* capability, such as **li** (number of lines). `tgetnum` returns the numerical value or –1, if the capability is not found in the terminal entry. All numerical *termcap* entries are non-negative, so –1 unambiguously indicates a missing entry.

`tgetstr` locates string-type capabilities and is called with two arguments: the capability name *cap*, such as *cl* (clear screen), and the *address* of a buffer pointer, *bp*. `tgetstr` extracts the given string and copies it to the buffer, replacing all quoted escape sequences with actual values and terminating the string with a null. (For example, the two characters "\E" in *termcap* are replaced by the single ESCAPE character.) If the capability is found, `tgetstr` returns a pointer to the string; otherwise, it returns NULL.

The buffer usage by tgetstr is tricky and deserves closer scrutiny. First, note that argument bp is the address of a pointer to the buffer (that is, a pointer to a pointer). Before calling tgetstr, you should allocate a buffer large enough to contain all the string values you wish to evaluate: 1024 bytes is a good size to use. A pointer to this buffer should then be set, and the *address* of this pointer passed each time to tgetstr. tgetstr updates the pointer after each call, to point to the next available location in the buffer.

The following code fragment shows how this might be done:

```
char stringbuf[1024];       /* allocate a buffer */
char *bufptr;               /* a buffer pointer */
char *home, *clear, *move;/* some capabilities to set */

/* call tgetent( ) to read entry first ... */

bufptr = stringbuf;              /* set pointer to buffer */
home = tgetstr("ho", &bufptr); /* get home string */
clear = tgetstr("cl", &bufptr);/* get clear string */
move = tgetstr("cm", &bufptr); /* get cursor motion string */
```

The cursor motion string returned by tgetstr *("cm", ...)* contains codes that indicate how column and line values are to be substituted. The routine tgoto decodes these values for a particular location: it is passed the cursor motion string *cm*, the column number *col*, and the line number *lin*. It returns a pointer to a control string that, when sent to the terminal with tputs, moves the cursor to that column and line. If the *cm* string does not make sense, or if *col* or *lin* is out of bounds, tgoto will print the obscure error message "oops".

tgoto does not protect against strings containing tab characters, and it is up to the programmer to ensure that the terminal driver does not replace tabs with strings of spaces. This can be accomplished through a UNIX system terminal ioctl call. Details of this call vary between UNIX systems: on those derived from UNIX System V, the TAB3 bit must be turned off in the *c_cflag* member of the *termio* structure; in UNIX systems derived from V7 (which includes BSD 4.3), the *XTABS* bit must be turned off in the *sg_flags* member of the *sgtty* structure. See your UNIX system documentation for more details.

`tputs` is used to output strings to the terminal with appropriate padding. Its arguments are: *cp*, the capability string or a cursor motion string returned by `tgoto`; *affcnt*, the number of lines affected by the command; and *outc*, a pointer to a function that takes a single *char* and outputs it to the terminal. The *affcnt* value is used to calculate padding that is proportional to the number of lines operated on and should be 1 for those capabilities that are not line-oriented.

`tputs` relies on two external variables when calculating padding: PC, the padding character (or null by default), and `ospeed`, the terminal output speed. The programmer must set these variables before calling `tputs`. PC can be taken from a `tgetstr` call (but note that it is a `char` variable, not a `char *`); `ospeed` is determined from an `ioctl` call to the terminal driver. See your UNIX system documentation for a description of the latter.

It is a common source of error for a programmer to avoid calling `tputs` and simply use `printf` or other such routine to write a capability string. This use will fail on strings that contain padding information, since the padding numbers will be sent literally to the screen.

Another common error is to try to skip past (or interpret) the padding information before sending the string to `tputs`. This fails in two cases: when the padding really **has** to be sent to the terminal, or when using the *termcap* emulation provided with *terminfo*, in which case the padding information is specified using the $<n> syntax.

Test Program

A test program written for a BSD 4.3 system using these routines follows. It initializes a number of variables, clears the screen, and uses cursor motion sequences to position the cursor at each cell on the screen and write a ''*''. When finished, it clears the screen.

The program is compiled with the command:

```
% cc -o prog prog.c -ltermlib
```

Your system may require *-ltermcap* or *-lcurses* rather than *-ltermlib*.

```
#include <stdio.h>
#include <sgtty.h>

char *tgetstr( );
char *tgoto( );
char *getenv( );

extern char *tgetstr(), *tgoto(), *getenv();
extern int tgetent(), tgetflag(), tgetnum(), tputs();
extern char PC, *PC, *UP;
extern short ospeed;

main( ){
        char entrybuf[1024];     /* buffer for entry */
        char stringbuf[1024];    /* allocate a buffer */
        char *bufptr;            /* a buffer pointer */
        char *s;
        int lines, columns;      /* # of lines and columns */
        char *clear, *move;      /* some strings */
        char *term;              /* terminal name */
        int  outc( );            /* routine to write a character */
        struct sgttyb sgbuf;
        int i, j;

        if( (term = getenv("TERM")) == NULL )/* get TERM type */
            fatal("TERM is not set.");

        ioctl(0, TIOCGETP, &sgbuf);    /* get tty settings */
        sgbuf.sg_flags &= ~XTABS;      /* turn off tab expansion */
        ospeed = sgbuf.sg_ospeed;      /* get output speed */
        ioctl(0, TIOCSETP, &sgbuf);    /* set new tty settings */

        if( tgetent( entrybuf, term) != 1 )  /* read in entry */
            fatal("Error locating entry.");

        lines = tgetnum("li");    /* get number of lines */
        columns = tgetnum("co");  /* get number of columns */

        bufptr = stringbuf;
        clear = tgetstr("cl", &bufptr);/* get clear string */
        move = tgetstr("cm", &bufptr); /* get cursor motion
                                        * string */

        if( (s = tgetstr("pc", &bufptr)) != NULL )
            PC = *s;
        BC = tgetstr("bc", &bufptr);
        UP = tgetstr("up", &bufptr);
```

```
    /* clear screen */

    if( clear == NULL )
        fatal("clear string is not set\n");
    tputs(clear, 1, outc);

    if( move == NULL )
        fatal ("cursor motion string is not set\n");

    for( i = 0; i < lines; ++i ){
        for( j = 0; j < columns; ++j ){
        /* avoid writing to bottom right-hand corner */
            if(i == lines - 1 && j == columns - 1 )
                continue;
            s = tgoto(move, j, i);
            tputs(s, 1, outc);
            putchar('*');
        }
    }
    tputs(clear, 1, outc);
}

/* write out one character */

outc(c)
int c;
{
    putchar(c);
}

/* print an error message and exit */

fatal(message)
char *message;
{
    fprintf(stderr, "%s\n", message);
    exit(1);
}
```

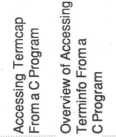

C

Accessing Terminfo From a C Program

The Terminfo Routines
Test Program
Capability Variable Names

This appendix is an overview of how to use *terminfo* in your programs. It is intended for C programmers.

As with *termcap*, there are two ways to use *terminfo* in your programs:

* *curses*

    The *curses* library contains a complete set of routines for managing a screen display. *curses* routines use information extracted from the *terminfo* database and provide a convenient interface to the programmer. The *curses* routines attempt to optimize terminal output by determining the most efficient methods for moving the cursor or updating the display. They also are clever enough to seek alternate methods for an operation if a particular capability does not exist.

curses routines are recommended as a general purpose interface to *terminfo*, since they free the programmer from the nitty gritty details of the terminal database. *curses* is described in the Nutshell Handbook, *Programming with Curses*, and in the reference pages of your system documentation.

- *terminfo routines*

  As was the case with *termcap*, you find that *curses* routines are too large or otherwise inappropriate to your task, or if you simply wish to experience the exhilaration of accomplishing a simple task in a difficult way, then use the lower-level routines. Although these are stored in the *curses* library, and used by *curses* to extract *terminfo* capability information, they are logically a lower-level interface. By calling these routines through your own program, you gain direct access to the database at the expense of additional programming complexity. You also gain access to certain capability strings, such as function key programming, which may not be available through *curses*.

The Terminfo Routines

To use the routines, you must compile with the *-lcurses* option. You must also include the two header files *<curses.h>* and *<term.h>* in your program, as they contain the string, number and flag definitions used by *terminfo*. The library routines are as follows and should be properly declared in each program that uses them.

Function and Arguments	Description
`char *getenv(var)` `char *var`	Get value of environment variable `var`.

`setupterm(term, fd, rc)`
`char *term`
`int fd`
`int *rc`
	Read in entry and initialize.
	Terminal type.
	Output file descriptor.
	Address of status word.

`char *tparm(str, p1,`
   `p2, . . . p9)`
`char *str`
`long p1, p2 , . . . p9`
	Substitute arguments in capability string.
	Capability string.
	Parameters.

`tputs (cp, affcnt, outc)`
`char *cp`
`int affcnt`
`int (*outc)( )`
	Output a string with padding.
	Capability string.
	Number of lines affected.
	Function to output each character.

`putp(str)`
 	
`char *str`
	Convenient front-end to `tputs` through `putchar`.
	Capability string.

`vidputs(attrs, putc)`
`int attrs;`
`int (*outc)( )`
	Set video attributes.
	Attribute value.
	Function to output each character.

`vidattr(attrs)`	Convenient front-end to `vidputs` through `putchar`.
`def_prog_mde`	Save current tty modes.

`getenv` returns a pointer to a character string that contains the value of an environment variable. In the context of *terminfo* programming, it is called with the argument "TERM" to determine the name of your terminal type and returns a pointer to a string such as "vt100". This pointer must be saved and used as the *name* argument to a subsequent `setupterm` call. `getenv` is actually found in the standard C library, not in the *terminfo* library, but it is described here since it is so frequently used with *terminfo*.

Once the terminal type is determined with `getenv`, `setupterm` must be called to read in the *terminfo* database entry and initializes the terminal. The arguments are: *term*, the terminal type (returned by `getenv`); *fd*, the file descriptor on which output should take place (usually file descriptor 1, standard output); and *rc*, the address of a status integer, or `(int*)NULL` if no status is desired. Note that `setupterm` does not return a value to indicate its success but instead deposits a value in the integer pointed to by `rc`. A value of 1 indicates success; the most likely reason for failure is that a *terminfo* entry cannot be found for the named terminal.

`setupterm` looks for the terminal entry under the system default terminfo directory */usr/lib/terminfo*. However, this choice may be overridden through the environment variable TERMINFO, which indicates an alternate directory to search for terminal entries. This variable is most commonly set in your shell's login initialization file and provides a convenient method for maintaining a private set of *terminfo* entries for use when debugging or when you have no permission to modify entries in the */usr/lib/terminfo* directory. A null character pointer may also be passed for the *term* parameter, in which case `setupterm` will invoke `getenv` for you. The simplest usage of `setupterm` is thus:

```
setupterm ((char*)0, 1, (int*)0);
```

Once you have initialized your terminal through `setupterm`, you are able to access all capabilities (unlike the *termcap* routines, which require you to invoke `tgetflag`, `tgetnum`, and `tgetstr` for each capability to be used). The names of these capabilities can be found at the end of this appendix, in the *terminfo* reference pages of your system, and on-line within the file */usr/include/term.h*. The names tend to be self-explanatory, for example `clear_screen`, `cursor_address`, or `lines`.

Certain capability values are parameterized. For example, `cursor_address` needs a line/column pair, and `set_attributes` needs values for each video attribute to be set. These parameters are substituted through the routine `tparm`, which is passed the capability name and up to nine arguments. The interpretation of these arguments is dependent on the capability: for example, `cursor_address` takes a line number followed by a column number. `tparm` returns the string which, when sent to the terminal via tputs, will perform the operation with the indicated values.

tputs is used to output strings to the terminal with appropriate padding. Its arguments are: *cp*, the capability string or return string from tparm; *affcnt*, the number of lines affected by the command; and *outc*, a pointer to a function that takes a single *char* and outputs it to the terminal. The *affcnt* value is used to calculate padding that is proportional to the number of lines operated on, and should be 1 for those capabilities that are not line-oriented.

It is a common source of error for a programmer to avoid calling tputs and simply use printf or another such routine to write a capability string. This use will fail on strings which contain padding information, since the padding numbers will be sent literally to the screen.

The most common use of tputs is with an *affcnt* value of 1, and an *outc* function equivalent to putchar which writes one character to standard output. The routine putp provides a convenient way of handling this case and need only be passed a capability string.

terminfo provides control for a number of different video attributes, and the routine vidputs to set them. vidputs is passed two arguments: *attrs*, a bit-mask of the attributes to be set, and *outc*, a pointer to a function that takes a single *char* and outputs it to the terminal. Possible attribute values are as follows.

Attribute	Description
A_STANDOUT	Most visible highlighting mode.
A_UNDERLINE	Underline mode.
A_REVERSE	Reverse video mode.
A_BLINK	Blink mode.
A_DIM	Half-intensity mode.
A_BOLD	Bright mode.
A_PROTECT	Protected no-overwrite mode.
A_ALTCHARSET	Alternate (often graphics) character set.

For example, to turn on "bold" and "blinking" modes:

```
vidputs(A_BOLD|A_BLINK, outc)
```

Note that most terminals do not support all attributes, and results are inconsistent between different terminals when multiple attributes are combined.

The most common usage of `vidputs` is with an *outc* function which operates like `putchar` to send one character to standard output. In this case, use the convenient function `vidattr`, which is passed only an attributes argument.

Two routines are provided to control the UNIX system terminal driver modes: `resetterm` and `fixterm`. `resetterm` restores the original terminal driver modes that were set before program entry. This should be called just before your program exits or before any escape to an interactive shell. `fixterm` sets the modes needed for using *terminfo*. It is called automatically by `setupterm` upon startup, and need only be used following a `resetterm` when returning from a shell escape.

Test Program

A test program using these routines follows. It initializes a number of variables, clears the screen, and uses cursor motion sequences to position the cursor at each cell on the screen and write a "*". When finished, it clears the screen.

The program is compiled with the command:

```
$ cc -o prog prog.c -lcurses
```

```
#include <curses.h>
#include <term.h>

char *tparm( );
char *getenv( );

main( ) {
```

```
      char *term;      /* terminal name */
      int   outc( );   /* routine to write a character */
      int status;
      int i, j;
      char *s;
      /* get TERM type */
      if( (term = getenv("TERM")) == NULL )
            fatal("TERM is not set.");

      setupterm(term, 1, &status);
      if( status != 1 )
            fatal("Error in setupterm");

      /* clear screen */

      if( clear_screen == NULL )
            fatal("clear string is not set\n");
      putp(clear_screen);

      if( cursor_address == NULL )
            fatal ("cursor motion string is not set\n");

      for( i = 0; i < lines; ++i ){
            for( j = 0; j < columns; ++j ){
                  /* avoid writing to bottom right-hand corner */
                  if(i == lines - 1 && j == columns - 1 )
                        continue;
                  s = tparm(cursor_address, i, j);
                  putp(s);
                  putchar('*');
            }
      }
      putp(clear_screen);
}

/* print an error message and exit */

fatal(message)
char *message;
{
      fprintf(stderr, "%s\n", message);
      exit(1);
}
```

Capability Variable Names

The following table lists the C variable names (in courier font) corresponding to *terminfo* capabilities.

acsc	acs_chars	*ed*	clr_eos
am	auto_right_margin	*el*	clr_eol
bel	bell	*ell*	clr_bol
blink	enter_blink_mode	*enacs*	ena_acs
bold	enter_bold_mode	*eo*	erase_overstrike
bw	auto_left_margin	*eslok*	status_line_esc_ok
cbt	back_tab	*ff*	form_feed
chts	hard_cursor	*flash*	flash_screen
civis	cursor_invisible	*fsl*	from_status_line
clear	clear_screen	*gn*	generic_type
cmdch	command_character	*hc*	hard_copy
cnorm	cursor_normal	*hd*	down_half_line
cols	columns	*home*	cursor_home
cr	carriage_return	*hpa*	column_address
csr	change_scroll_region	*hs*	has_status_line
cub	parm_left_cursor	*ht*	tab
cub1	cursor_left	*hts*	set_tab
cud	parm_down_cursor	*hu*	up_half_line
cud1	cursor_down	*hz*	tilde_glitch
cuf	parm_right_cursor	*ich*	parm_ich
cuf1	cursor_right	*ich1*	insert_character
cup	cursor_address	*if*	init_file
cuu	parm_up_cursor	*il*	parm_insert_line
cuu1	cursor_up	*il1*	insert_line
cvvis	cursor_visible	*in*	insert_null_glitch
da	memory_above	*ind*	scroll_forward
db	memory_below	*indn*	parm_index
dch	parm_dch	*invis*	enter_secure_mode
dch1	delete_character	*ip*	insert_padding
dim	enter_dim_mode	*iprog*	init_prog
dl	parm_delete_line	*is1*	init_1string
dl1	delete_line	*is2*	init_2string
dsl	dis_status_line	*is3*	init_3string
ech	erase_chars	*it*	init_tabs

kBEG	key_sbeg	*kcpy*	key_copy
kCAN	key_scancel	*kcrt*	key_create
kCMD	key_scommand	*kctab*	key_ctab
kCPY	key_scopy	*kcub1*	key_left
kCRT	key_screate	*kcud1*	key_down
kDC	key_sdc	*kcuf1*	key_right
kDL	key_sdl	*kcuu1*	key_up
kEND	key_send	*kdch1*	key_dc
kEOL	key_seol	*kdll*	key_dl
kEXT	key_sexit	*ked*	key_eos
kFND	key_sfind	*kel*	key_eol
kHLP	key_shelp	*kend*	key_end
kHOM	key_shome	*kent*	key_enter
kIC	key_sic	*kext*	key_exit
kLFT	key_sleft	*kf0*	key_f0
kMOV	key_smove	*kf1*	key_f1
kMSG	key_smessage	...	...
kNXT	key_snext	*kf9*	key_f9
kOPT	key_soptions	*kf10*	key_f10
kPRT	key_sprint	...	...
kPRV	key_sprevious	*kf63*	key_f63
kRDO	key_sredo	*kfnd*	key_find
kRES	key_srsume	*khlp*	key_help
kRIT	key_sright	*khome*	key_home
kRPL	key_sreplace	*khts*	key_stab
kSAV	key_ssave	*kich1*	key_ic
kSPD	key_ssuspend	*kil1*	key_il
kUND	key_sundo	*kind*	key_sf
ka1	key_a1	*kll*	key_ll
ka3	key_a3	*km*	has_meta_key
kb2	key_b2	*kmov*	key_move
kbeg	key_beg	*kmrk*	key_mark
kbs	key_backspace	*kmsg*	key_message
kc1	key_c1	*knp*	key_npage
kc3	key_c3	*knxt*	key_next
kcan	key_cancel	*kopn*	key_open
kcbt	key_btab	*kopt*	key_options
kclo	key_close	*kpp*	key_ppage
kclr	key_clear	*kprt*	key_print
kcmd	key_command	*kprv*	key_previous

krdo	key_redo	*pfloc*	pkey_local
kref	key_reference	*pfx*	pkey_xmit
kres	key_resume	*pln*	plab_norm
krfr	key_refresh	*prot*	enter_protected_mode
kri	key_sr	*rc*	restore_cursor
krmir	key_eic	*rep*	repeat_char
krpl	key_replace	*rev*	enter_reverse_mode
krst	key_restart	*rf*	reset_file
ksav	key_save	*rfi*	req_for_input
kslt	key_select	*ri*	scroll_reverse
kspd	key_suspend	*rin*	parm_rindex
ktbc	key_catab	*rmacs*	exit_alt_charset_mode
kund	key_undo	*rmam*	exit_am_mode
lf0	lab_f0	*rmcup*	exit_ca_mode
lf1	lab_f1	*rmdc*	exit_delete_mode
...	...	*rmir*	exit_insert_mode
lf10	lab_f10	*rmkx*	keypad_local
lh	label_height	*rmln*	label_off
lines	lines	*rmm*	meta_off
ll	cursor_to_ll	*rmp*	char_padding
lm	lines_of_memory	*rmso*	exit_standout_mode
lw	label_width	*rmul*	exit_underline_mode
mc0	print_screen	*rmxon*	exit_xon_mode
mc4	prtr_off	*rs1*	reset_1string
mc5	prtr_on	*rs2*	reset_2string
mc5i	prtr_silent	*rs3*	reset_3string
mc5p	prtr_non	*sc*	save_cursor
mgc	clear_margins	*sgr*	set_attributes
mir	move_insert_mode	*sgr0*	exit_attribute_mode
mrcup	cursor_mem_address	*smacs*	enter_alt_charset_mode
msgr	move_standout_mode	*smam*	enter_am_mode
nel	newline	*smcup*	enter_ca_mode
nlab	num_labels	*smdc*	enter_delete_mode
npc	no_pad_char	*smgl*	set_left_margin
nrrmc	non_rev_rmcup	*smgr*	set_right_margin
nxon	needs_xon_xoff	*smir*	enter_insert_mode
os	over_strike	*smkx*	keypad_xmit
pad	pad_char	*smln*	label_on
pb	padding_baud_rate	*smm*	meta_on
pfkey	pkey_key	*smso*	enter_standout_mode

smul	enter_underline_mode
smxon	enter_xon_mode
tbc	clear_all_tabs
tsl	to_status_line
uc	underline_char
ul	transparent_underline
vpa	row_address
vt	virtual_terminal
wind	set_window
wsl	width_status_line
xenl	eat_newline_glitch
xhp	ceol_standout_glitch
xmc	magic_cookie_glitch
xoffc	xoff_character
xon	xon_xoff
xonc	xon_character
xsb	no_esc_ctlc
xt	dest_tabs_magic_smso

Capabilities Used by vi

Accessing Termcap
From a C Program

Overview of Accessing
Terminfo From a
C Program

List of Capabilities

D

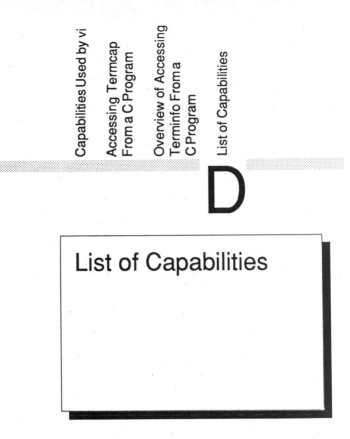

List of Capabilities

The following table lists all *termcap* and *terminfo* capabilities. The capabilities are listed alphabetically in the first column, regardless of whether they belong to *termcap* or *terminfo*. You can distinguish which database they belong to because they follow the standard font conventions: **bold** indicating *termcap* and ***bold italic*** indicating *terminfo*. The table also lists the equivalent *termcap* or *terminfo* capability (if any), a brief description, and the chapter where the capability is discussed further.

Capability	Equivalent	Description	Chapter
!1=	kSAV=	Describe shifted save key.	12
!2=	kSPD=	Describe shifted suspend key.	12
!3=	kUND=	Describe shifted undo key.	12
#1=	kHLP=	Describe shifted help key.	12
#2=	kHOM=	Describe shifted home key.	12
#3=	kIC=	Describe shifted input key.	12
#4=	kLFT=	Describe shifted left arrow key.	12
%0=	krdo=	Describe redo key.	12
%1=	khelp=	Describe help key.	12
%2=	kmrk=	Describe mark key.	12
%3=	kmsg=	Describe message key.	12
%4=	kmov=	Describe move key.	12
%5=	knxt=	Describe next-object key.	12
%6=	kopn=	Describe open key.	12
%7=	kopt=	Describe options key.	12
%8=	kprv=	Describe previous-object key.	12
%9=	kprt=	Describe print or copy key.	12
&0=	kCAN=	Describe shifted cancel key.	12
&1=	kref=	Describe reference key.	12
&2=	krfr=	Describe refresh key.	12
&3=	krpl=	Describe replace key.	12
&4=	krst=	Describe restart key.	12
&5=	kres=	Describe resume key.	12
&6=	ksav=	Describe save key.	12
&7=	kspd=	Describe suspend key.	12
&8=	kund=	Describe undo key.	12
&9=	kBEG=	Describe shifted beginning key.	12
*0=	kFND=	Describe shifted find key.	12
*1=	kCMD=	Describe shifted command key.	12
*2=	kCPY=	Describe shifted copy key.	12
*3=	kCRT=	Describe shifted create key.	12
*4=	kDC=	Describe shifted delete-char key.	12
*5=	kDL=	Describe shifted delete-line key.	12
*6=	kslt=	Describe select key.	12
*7=	kEND=	Describe shifted end key.	12
*8=	kEOL=	Describe shifted clear-line key.	12
*9=	kEXT=	Describe shifted exit key.	12
@0=	kfnd=	Describe find key.	12
@1=	kbeg=	Describe beginning key.	12
@2=	kcan=	Describe cancel key.	12
@3=	kclo=	Describe close key.	12

Capability	Equivalent	Description	Chapter
@4=	*kcmd=*	Describe command key.	12
@5=	*kcpy=*	Describe copy key.	12
@6=	*kcrt=*	Describe create key.	12
@7=	*kend=*	Describe end key.	12
@8=	*kent=*	Describe enter/send key.	12
@9=	*kext=*	Describe exit key.	12
5i	*mc5i*	Printer will not echo on the screen (not in BSD 4.3).	14
%a=	*kMSG=*	Describe shifted message key.	12
ac=	*acsc=*	Map line drawing character set to ASCII characters (not in BSD 4.3).	14
acsc=	ac=	Map line drawing character set to ASCII characters (not in BSD 4.3).	14
ae=	*rmacs=*	End using alternate character set.	11
al=	*il1=*	Add line below line with cursor.	9
AL=	*il=*	Add #1 lines above line with cursor.	9
am	*am*	Terminal does automargin (wraparound).	16
as=	*smacs=*	Start using alternate character set.	11
%b=	*kMOV=*	Describe shifted move key.	12
bc=	None	Backspace if not ^H (obsolete).	12
bel=	bl=	Audio bell: make terminal noise. Usually ^G.	11
bl=	*bel=*	Audio bell: make terminal noise. Usually ^G.	11
blink=	mb=	Turn on blinking attribute.	11
bold=	md=	Turn on bold (extra-bright) attribute.	11
bs	None	Terminal uses ^H to backspace (obsolete).	8
bt=	*cbt=*	Back tab: move to previous tab stop.	10
bw	*bw*	Backwards wrap, backspacing off left edge. Wraps cursor to right edge, previous line.	16
%c=	*kNXT=*	Describe shifted next key.	12
cb=	*el1=*	Clear from beginning of line to cursor (not in BSD 4.3).	9
cbt=	bt=	Back tab: move to previous tab stop.	10
CC=	*cmdch=*	Command character: dummy command character in string commands, replaced at run time with CC environment variable.	16
cd=	*ed=*	Clear display after cursor.	9

Capa-bility	Equiv-alent	Description	Chap-ter
ce=	_el=_	Clear to end of line.	9
ch=	_hpa=_	Move cursor horizontally on its line to column #1.	8
chts	HC	Cursor hard to see when not on bottom line (not in BSD 4.3).	11
civis=	vi=	Make cursor invisible.	11
cl=	_clear=_	Clear screen. Cursor to upper left.	9
clear=	cl=	Clear screen. Cursor to upper left.	9
cm=	_cup=_	Move cursor to row #1 and column #2 (absolutely essential).	8
CM=	_mrcup=_	Move cursor to row #1 and column #2 relative to the memory.	8
cmdch=	CC=	Command character: dummy command character in string commands, replaced at run time with CC environment variable.	16
cnorm=	ve=	Make cursor normal (undo effect of **vs=** and **vi**).	11
co#	_cols#_	The number of columns on the screen.	8
cols#	co#	The number of columns on the screen.	8
cr=	_cr=_	Carriage return if not ^M.	12
cs=	_csr=_	Change scrolling region of screen to rows #1 to #2.	8
csr=	cs=	Change scrolling region of screen to rows #1 to #2.	8
ct=	_tbc=_	Clear all tab stops.	10
cub=	LE=	Move cursor left a number of columns.	8
cub1=	le=	Move cursor left.	8
cud=	DO=	Move cursor down a number of rows.	8
cud1=	do=	Move cursor down.	8
cuf=	RI=	Move cursor right a number of columns.	8
cuf1=	nd=	Non-destructive space (cursor moves to right).	8
cup=	cm=	Move cursor to row #1 and column #2 (absolutely essential).	8
cuu=	UP=	Move cursor up a number of rows.	8
cuu1=	up=	Move cursor up.	8
cv=	_vpa=_	Move cursor vertically in its column to line #1.	8
cvvis=	vs=	Make cursor very visible.	11

Capability	Equivalent	Description	Chapter
%d=	kOPT=	Describe shifted options key.	12
da	da	Display retained above screen (usually multi-page terminals).	8
db	db	Display retained below screen (usually multi-page terminals).	8
dB#	None	Delay (in milliseconds) for backspace on hardcopy terminal (obsolete).	14
dc=	dch1=	Delete character at cursor. Must be defined if delete mode defined.	9
dC#	None	Delay (in milliseconds) for carriage return on hardcopy terminal (obsolete).	14
DC=	dch=	Delete #1 characters starting at cursor.	9
dch=	DC=	Delete #1 characters starting at cursor.	9
dch1=	dc=	Delete character at cursor. Must be defined if delete mode defined.	9
dF#	None	Delay (in milliseconds) for formfeed on hardcopy terminal (obsolete).	14
dim=	mh=	Turn on dim (half-bright) attribute.	11
dl=	dl1=	Delete line that cursor is on.	9
DL=	dl=	Delete #1 lines including and below line with cursor.	9
dl1=	dl=	Delete line that cursor is on.	9
dm=	smdc=	Begin delete mode.	9
dN#	None	Delay (in milliseconds) for newline on hardcopy terminal (obsolete).	14
do=	cud1=	Move cursor down.	8
DO=	cud=	Move cursor down a number of rows.	8
ds=	dsl=	Disable status: turns off or erases the status line.	8
dsl=	ds=	Disable status: turns off or erases the status line.	8
dT#	None	Delay (in milliseconds) for tab on hardcopy terminal (obsolete).	14
dV#	None	Delay (in milliseconds) for vertical tab on hardcopy terminal (obsolete).	14
%e=	kPRV=	Describe shifted prev key.	12
eA=	enacs=	Enable alternate character set (not in BSD 4.3).	11
ec=	ech=	"Erase" #1 characters starting at cursor.	9

Capability	Equivalent	Description	Chapter
ech=	ec=	"Erase" #1 characters starting at cursor.	9
ed=	rmdc=	End delete mode.	9
ed=	cd=	Clear display after cursor.	9
ei=	rmir=	End insert mode.	9
el=	ce=	Clear to end of line.	9
ell=	cb=	Clear from beginning of line to cursor (not in BSD 4.3).	9
enacs=	eA=	Enable alternate character set (not in BSD 4.3).	11
eo	eo	A space erases all characters at cursor even though terminal overstrikes.	16
EP	None	Even parity (obsolete).	16
es	eslok	Escape sequences and special characters work in status line.	8
eslok	es	Escape sequences and special characters work in status line.	8
%f=	kPRT=	Describe shifted print key.	12
F1=	kf11=	The string sent by function key f11.	12
F2=	kf12=	The string sent by function key f12.	12
F3=	kf13=	The string sent by function key f13.	12
F9=	kf19=	The string sent by function key f19.	12
Fa=	kf46=	The string sent by function key f46.	12
FA=	kf20=	The string sent by function key f20.	12
Fb=	kf47=	The string sent by function key f47.	12
FB=	kf21=	The string sent by function key f21.	12
Fc=	kf48=	The string sent by function key f48.	12
FC=	kf22=	The string sent by function key f22.	12
ff=	ff=	Formfeed character on hardcopy terminals if not ^L.	14
flash=	vb=	Visual bell: flash terminal screen.	11
Fq=	kf62=	The string sent by function key f62.	12
Fr=	kf63=	The string sent by function key f63.	12
fs=	fsl=	From status: return cursor to its position before going to status line.	8
fsl=	fs=	From status: return cursor to its position before going to status line.	8
FY=	kf44=	The string sent by function key f44.	12
FZ=	kf45=	The string sent by function key f45.	12

Capa-bility	Equiv-alent	Description	Chap-ter
%g=	*kRDO=*	Describe **shifted redo** key.	12
gn	*gn*	Generic terminal descriptions for dialup, switch, patch, network, etc.	16
%h=	*kRPL=*	Describe **shifted replace** key.	12
hc	*hc*	Terminal is a hardcopy terminal.	14
HC	*chts*	Cursor hard to see when not on bottom line (not in BSD 4.3).	11
hd=	*hd=*	Halfline down: move cursor down half a linefeed.	8
HD	None	Half duplex (obsolete).	16
ho=	*home=*	Move cursor home (upper lefthand corner).	8
home=	ho=	Move cursor home (upper lefthand corner).	8
hpa=	ch=	Move cursor horizontally on its line to column #1.	8
hs	*hs*	Terminal has status line.	8
ht=	ta=	Tab: move to next hardware tab stop (usually ^I).	10
hts=	st=	Set a tab stop in all rows, current column.	10
hu=	*hu=*	Halfline up: move cursor up half a linefeed.	8
hz	*hz*	Hazeltine glitch: cannot print tildes ("~").	14
%l=	*kRIT=*	Describe shifted right arrow key.	12
i1=	*is1=*	Init string 1: initialize terminal at login.	10
i3=	*is3=*	Init string 3: initialize terminal at login.	10
ic=	*ich1=*	Insert character: open a space so that the next character after this string can be inserted.	9
IC=	*ich=*	Parameterized character insert: open up #1 spaces for characters to be inserted into.	9
ich=	IC=	Parameterized character insert: open up #1 spaces for characters to be inserted into.	9
ich1=	ic=	Insert character: open a space so that the next character after this string can be inserted.	9

Capability	Equivalent	Description	Chapter
if=	*if=*	Initialization file containing long initialization strings.	10
il=	*AL=*	Add #1 lines above line with cursor.	9
il1=	al=	Add line below line with cursor.	9
im=	*smir=*	Begin insert mode.	9
in	in	Terminal inserts nulls, not spaces, to fill whitespace in screen.	9
ind=	sf=	Scroll forward one line.	8
indn=	SF=	Scroll forward #1 lines.	8
invis=	mk=	Turn on blanking attribute (characters invisible).	11
ip=	*ip=*	Insert pad: pad time and any special characters needed after inserting a character in insert mode.	9
iP=	*iprog=*	Init program: initialize terminal at login.	10
iprog=	iP=	Init program: initialize terminal at login.	10
is=	*is2=*	Initialization string for terminal initialization.	10
is1=	i1=	Init string 1: initialize terminal at login.	10
is2=	is=	Init string 2: initialize terminal at login.	10
is3=	i3=	Init string 3: initialize terminal at login.	10
it#	it#	Initial number of spaces between tabs.	10
%j=	*kRES=*	Describe shifted resume key.	12
k;=	*kf10=*	The string sent by the eleventh function key (labeled f10).	12
k0=	*kf0=*	The string sent by the zeroth function key (labeled f10).	12
k1=	*kf1=*	The string sent by the first function key (labeled f1).	12
K1=	*ka1=*	Sent by upper left key of keypad.	12
k2=	*kf2=*	The string sent by the second function key (labeled f2).	12
K2=	*kb2=*	Sent by upper right key of keypad.	12
K3=	*ka3=*	Sent by center key of keypad.	12
K4=	*kc1=*	Sent by lower left key of keypad.	12
K5=	*kc3=*	Sent by lower right key of keypad.	12

Capability	Equivalent	Description	Chapter
k9=	kf9=	The string sent by the ninth function key (labeled f9).	12
ka=	ktbc=	String sent by **clear all tabs** key.	12
kA=	kill=	String sent by **insert line** key.	12
ka1=	K1=	Sent by upper left key of keypad.	12
ka3=	K3=	Sent by center key of keypad.	12
kb=	kbs=	String sent by **backspace** key.	12
kB=	kcbt=	String sent by **back tab** key (not in BSD 4.3).	12
kb2=	K2=	Sent by upper right key of keypad.	12
kbeg=	@1=	Describe **beginning** key.	12
kBEG=	&9=	Describe **shifted beginning** key.	12
kbs=	kb=	String sent by **backspace** key.	12
kC=	kclr=	String sent by **clear screen** or **erase** key.	12
kc1=	K4=	Sent by lower left key of keypad.	12
kc3=	K5=	Sent by lower right key of keypad.	12
kcan=	@2=	Describe **cancel** key.	12
kCAN=	&0=	Describe **shifted cancel** key.	12
kcbt=	kB=	String sent by **back tab** key (not in BSD 4.3).	12
kclo=	@3=	Describe **close** key.	12
kclr=	kC=	String sent by **clear screen** or **erase** key.	12
kcmd=	@4=	Describe **command** key.	12
kCMD=	*1=	Describe **shifted command** key.	12
kcpy=	@5=	Describe **copy** key.	12
kCPY=	*2=	Describe **shifted copy** key.	12
kcrt=	@6=	Describe **create** key.	12
kCRT=	*3=	Describe **shifted create** key.	12
kctab=	kt=	String sent by **clear tab** key (in this column only).	12
kcub1=	kl=	Sent by left arrow key (corresponds to **bc=** or **bs**).	12
kcud1=	kd=	Sent by down arrow key (corresponds to *cud1=* and **do=**).	12
kcuf1=	kr=	Sent by right arrow key (corresponds to *cuf1=* and **nd=**).	12
kcuu1=	ku=	Sent by up arrow key (corresponds to *cuu1=* and **up=**).	12

Capability	Equivalent	Description	Chapter
kd=	*kcud1=*	Sent by down arrow key (corresponds to *cud1=* and do=).	12
kD=	*kdch1=*	String sent by delete character key.	12
kDC=	**4=*	Describe shifted delete-char key.	12
kdch1=	kD=	String sent by delete character key.	12
kDL=	**5=*	Describe shifted delete-line key.	12
kdll=	kL=	String sent by delete line key.	12
ke=	*rmkx=*	Turn keypad off, if can be turned on and off.	12
kE=	*kel=*	String sent by clear to end of line key.	12
ked=	kS=	String sent by clear to end of screen key.	12
kel=	kE=	String sent by clear to end of line key.	12
kend=	*@7=*	Describe end key.	12
kEND=	**7=*	Describe shifted end key.	12
kent=	*@8=*	Describe enter/send key.	12
kEOL=	**8=*	Describe shifted clear-line key.	12
kext=	*@9=*	Describe exit key.	12
kEXT=	**9=*	Describe shifted exit key.	12
kF=	*kind=*	String sent by scroll forward/down key.	12
kf0=	k0=	The string sent by the zeroth function key (labeled f10).	12
kf1=	k1=	The string sent by the first function key (labeled f1).	12
kf2=	k2=	The string sent by the second function key (labeled f2).	12
...	...		
kf9=	k9=	The string sent by the ninth function key (labeled f9).	12
kf10=	k;=	The string sent by the eleventh function key (labeled f10).	12
kf11=	F1=	The string sent by function key f11.	12
kf12=	F2=	The string sent by function key f12.	12
kf13=	F3=	The string sent by function key f13.	12
...	...		
kf19=	F9=	The string sent by function key f19.	12
kf20=	FA=	The string sent by function key f20.	12
kf21=	FB=	The string sent by function key f21.	12
kf22=	FC=	The string sent by function key f22.	12
...	...		

Capa-bility	Equiv-alent	Description	Chap-ter
kf44=	FY=	The string sent by function key f44.	12
kf45=	FZ=	The string sent by function key f45.	12
kf46=	Fa=	The string sent by function key f46.	12
kf47=	Fb=	The string sent by function key f47.	12
kf48=	Fc=	The string sent by function key f48.	12
...	...		
kf62=	Fq=	The string sent by function key f62.	12
kf63=	Fr=	The string sent by function key f63.	12
kfnd=	@0=	Describe **find** key.	12
kFND=	*0=	Describe **shifted find** key.	12
kh=	*khome=*	Sent by the home key (corresponds to *home=* and **ho=**).	12
kH=	*kll=*	String sent by **home-down** key (to lower left).	12
khelp=	%1=	Describe **help** key.	12
kHLP=	#1=	Describe **shifted help** key.	12
kHOM=	#2=	Describe **shifted home** key.	12
khome=	kh=	Sent by the home key (corresponds to *home=* and **ho=**).	12
khts=	kT=	String sent by **set tab stop** key (in this column).	12
kI=	*kich1=*	String sent by **insert character** or **enter insert mode** key.	12
kIC=	#3=	Describe **shifted input** key.	12
kich1=	kI=	String sent by **insert character** or **enter insert mode** key.	12
kill=	kA=	String sent by **insert line** key.	12
kind=	kF=	String sent by **scroll forward/down** key.	12
kl=	*kcub1=*	Sent by left arrow key (corresponds to **bc=**, **bs**, or **le=**).	12
kL=	*kdll=*	String sent by **delete line** key.	12
kLFT=	#4=	Describe **shifted left arrow** key.	12
kll=	kH=	String sent by **home-down** key (to lower left).	12
km	*km*	Terminal has a "meta" key.	14
kM=	*krmir=*	String sent by **exit insert mode** key.	12
kmov=	%4=	Describe **move** key.	12

Capa-bility	Equiv-alent	Description	Chap-ter
kmsg=	%3=	Describe message key.	12
kMSG=	%a=	Describe shifted message key.	12
kn#	None	The number of function keys defined.	12
kN=	knp=	String sent by next page key.	12
knp=	kN=	String sent by next page key.	12
knxt=	%5=	Describe next-object key.	12
kNXT=	%c=	Describe shifted next key.	12
ko=	None	"keys other": lists the cursor movement capabilities for which there is a defined key.	12
kopn=	%6=	Describe open key.	12
kopt=	%7=	Describe options key.	12
kOPT=	%d=	Describe shifted options key.	12
kP=	kpp=	String sent by previous page key.	12
kpp=	kP=	String sent by previous page key.	12
kprt=	%9=	Describe print or copy key.	12
kPRT=	%f=	Describe shifted print key.	12
kprv=	%8=	Describe previous-object key.	12
kPRV=	%e=	Describe shifted prev key.	12
kr=	kcuf1=	Sent by right arrow key (corresponds to cuf1= and nd=).	12
kR=	kri=	String sent by scroll backwards/up key.	12
krdo=	%0=	Describe redo key.	12
kRDO=	%g=	Describe shifted redo key.	12
kref=	&1=	Describe reference key.	12
kres=	&5=	Describe resume key.	12
kRES=	%j=	Describe shifted resume key.	12
krfr=	&2=	Describe refresh key.	12
kri=	kR=	String sent by scroll backwards/up key.	12
kRIT=	%i=	Describe shifted right arrow key.	12
krmir=	kM=	String sent by exit insert mode key.	12
krpl=	&3=	Describe replace key.	12
kRPL=	%h=	Describe shifted replace key.	12
krst=	&4=	Describe restart key.	12
ks=	smkx=	Turn keypad on, if can be turned on and off.	12
kS=	ked=	String sent by clear to end of screen key.	12
ksav=	&6=	Describe save key.	12
kSAV=	!1=	Describe shifted save key.	12
kslt=	*6=	Describe select key.	12

Capa-bility	Equiv-alent	Description	Chap-ter
kspd=	&7=	Describe **suspend** key.	12
kSPD=	!2=	Describe **shifted suspend** key.	12
kt=	*kctab=*	String sent by **clear tab** key (in this column only).	12
kT=	*khts=*	String sent by **set tab stop** key (in this column).	12
ktbc=	ka=	String sent by **clear all tabs** key.	12
ku=	*kcuu1=*	Sent by **up arrow** key (corresponds to *cuu1=* and **up=**).	12
kund=	&8=	Describe **undo** key.	12
kUND=	!3=	Describe **shifted undo** key.	12
l0=	*lf0=*	The label on the zeroth function key, if not f0.	12
l1=	*lf1=*	The label on the first function key, if not f1.	12
l2=	*lf2=*	The label on the second function key, if not f2.	12
...	...		
l9=	*lf9=*	The label on the ninth function key, if not f9.	12
la=	*lf10=*	The label on the tenth function key, if not f10.	12
LC	None	Lower case (obsolete).	16
le=	*cub1=*	Move cursor left.	8
LE=	*cub=*	Move cursor left a number of columns.	8
LF=	*rmln=*	Turn soft labels off (not in BSD 4.3).	12
lf0=	l0=	The label on the zeroth function key, if not f0.	12
lf1=	l1=	The label on the first function key, if not f1.	12
lf2=	l2=	The label on the second function key, if not f2.	12
lf9=	l9=	The label on the ninth function key, if not f9.	12
lf10=	la=	The label on the tenth function key, if not f10.	12
lh#	*lh#*	Height (number of columns) in each soft label (not in BSD 4.3).	12

Capa-bility	Equiv-alent	Description	Chap-ter
li#	*lines#*	The number of lines on the screen.	8
lines#	li#	The number of lines on the screen.	8
ll=	*ll=*	Move cursor to lower left corner.	8
lm#	*lm#*	Lines of memory: explicit 0 means varies.	16
LO=	*smln=*	Turn soft labels on (not in BSD 4.3).	12
lw#	*lw#*	Width (number of rows) in each soft label (not in BSD 4.3).	12
ma=	None	Map keypad to cursor movement for *vi* version 2.	12
mb=	*blink=*	Turn on blinking attribute.	11
MC=	*mgc=*	Clear soft margins (not in BSD 4.3).	10
mc0=	ps=	Print screen contents on auxiliary printer.	14
mc4=	pf=	Turn the printer off.	14
mc5=	po=	Turn the printer on.	14
mc5i	5i	Printer will not echo on the screen (not in BSD 4.3).	14
mc5p=	pO=	Turn the printer on for #1 bytes (#1 < 256).	14
md=	*bold=*	Turn on bold (extra-bright) attribute.	11
me=	*sgr0=*	Turn off all attributes.	11
mgc=	MC=	Clear soft margins (not in BSD 4.3).	10
mh=	*dim=*	Turn on dim (half-bright) attribute.	11
mi	*mir*	Terminal cursor movement commands work while in insert mode.	9
mir	mi	Terminal cursor movement commands work while in insert mode.	9
mk=	*invis=*	Turn on blanking attribute (characters invisible).	11
ml=	None	Memory lock: turn memory lock on above cursor (obsolete).	16
ML=	*smgl=*	Set left soft margin (not in BSD 4.3).	10
mm=	*smm=*	Meta mode on: put terminal into meta mode.	14
mo=	*rmm=*	Meta mode off: take terminal out of meta mode.	14
mp=	*prot=*	Turn on protected attribute.	11
mr=	*rev=*	Turn on reverse video attribute.	11
MR=	*smgr=*	Set right soft margin (not in BSD 4.3).	10

Capability	Equivalent	Description	Chapter
mrcup=	CM=	Move cursor to row #1 and column #2 relative to the memory.	8
ms	*msgr*	Move safe: can move cursor gracefully in standout or underline mode.	11
msgr	ms	Move safe: can move cursor gracefully in standout or underline mode.	11
mu=	None	Memory unlock: turn off memory lock above cursor (obsolete).	16
nc	None	No correctly working carriage return glitch (obsolete).	14
nd=	*cuf1=*	Non-destructive space (cursor moves to right).	8
nel=	nw=	Newline command (carriage return, then down).	8
nl=	None	Newline if not ^J (obsolete).	12
Nl#	*nlab#*	Number of soft labels available (not in BSD 4.3).	12
NL	None	\n is a newline, not a linefeed (obsolete).	16
nlab#	Nl#	Number of soft labels available (not in BSD 4.3).	12
NP	*npc*	No pad character (not in BSD 4.3).	13
npc	NP	No pad character (not in BSD 4.3).	13
NR	*nrrmc*	smcup= does not reverse *rmcup=* (not in BSD 4.3).	10
nrrmc	NR	smcup= does not reverse *rmcup=* (not in BSD 4.3).	10
ns	None	Abnormal scroll even though terminal is CRT (obsolete).	14
nw=	*nel=*	Newline command (carriage return, then down).	8
nx	*nxon*	No padding, must use XON/XOFF (not in BSD 4.3).	13
nxon	nx	No padding, must use XON/XOFF (not in BSD 4.3).	13
OP	None	Odd parity (obsolete).	16
os	*os*	Terminal can overstrike without erasing character.	16
pad=	pc=	Pad character if not NULL.	13

Capa-bility	Equiv-alent	Description	Chap-ter
pb#	*pb#*	Padding baud: no padding necessary at baud rate < **pb#**.	13
pc=	*pad=*	Pad character if not NULL.	13
pf=	*mc4=*	Turn the printer off.	14
pfkey=	pk=	Program key #1 to treat string #2 as if typed by user (mainly *terminfo*).	12
pfloc=	pl=	Program key #1 to execute string #2 in local mode (mainly *terminfo*).	12
pfx=	px=	Program key #1 to transmit string #2 to computer (mainly *terminfo*).	12
pk=	*pfkey=*	Program key #1 to treat string #2 as if typed by user (mainly *terminfo*).	12
pl=	*pfloc=*	Program key #1 to execute string #2 in local mode (mainly *terminfo*).	12
pln=	pn=	Program soft label #1 to show string #2 (not in BSD 4.3).	12
pn=	*pln=*	Program soft label #1 to show string #2 (not in BSD 4.3).	12
po=	*mc5=*	Turn the printer on.	14
pO=	*mc5p=*	Turn the printer on for #1 bytes (#1 < 256).	14
prot=	mp=	Turn on protected attribute.	11
ps=	*mc0=*	Print screen contents on auxiliary printer.	14
pt	None	Perform tabs: terminal has hardware tabs (obsolete).	10
px=	*pfx=*	Program key #1 to transmit string #2 to computer (mainly *terminfo*).	12
r1=	*rs1=*	Reset string 1: reset terminal to sane modes.	10
r2=	*rs2=*	Reset string 2: reset terminal to sane modes.	10
r3=	*rs3=*	Reset string 3: reset terminal to sane modes.	10
RA=	*rmam=*	Turn off automatic margins (not in BSD 4.3).	10
rc=	*rc=*	Restore cursor to position saved by sc=.	8
rep=	rp=	Repeat character #1 #2 times (predominantly *terminfo*).	9

Capa-bility	Equiv-alent	Description	Chap-ter
rev=	mr=	Turn on reverse video attribute.	11
rf=	*rf=*	Reset file containing long reset strings.	10
RF=	*rfi=*	Request for input: system ready for next input character (not in BSD 4.3).	16
rfi=	RF=	Request for input: system ready for next input character (not in BSD 4.3).	16
ri=	sr=	Scroll reverse (backwards) one line.	8
RI=	*cuf=*	Move cursor right a number of columns.	8
rin=	SR=	Scroll reverse (backwards) #1 lines.	8
rmacs=	ae=	End using alternate character set.	11
rmam=	RA=	Turn off automatic margins (not in BSD 4.3).	10
rmcup=	te=	End programs that use cursor motion.	10
rmdc=	ed=	End delete mode.	9
rmir=	ei=	End insert mode.	9
rmkx=	ke=	Turn keypad off, if can be turned on and off.	12
rmln=	LF=	Turn soft labels off (not in BSD 4.3).	12
rmm=	mo=	Meta mode off: take terminal out of meta mode.	14
rmp=	rP=	Padding after character typed in replace mode (not in BSD 4.3).	13
rmso=	se=	End standout mode.	11
rmul=	ue=	End underline mode.	11
rmxon=	RX=	Turn off XON/XOFF flow control (not in BSD 4.3).	13
rp=	*rep=*	Repeat character #1 #2 times (predominantly *terminfo*).	9
rP=	*rmp=*	Padding after character typed in replace mode (not in BSD 4.3).	13
rs=	None	Reset string: reset terminal to sane modes.	10
rs1=	r1=	Reset string 1: reset terminal to sane modes.	10
rs2=	r2=	Reset string 2: reset terminal to sane modes.	10
rs3=	r3=	Reset string 3: reset terminal to sane modes.	10

Capa-bility	Equiv-alent	Description	Chap-ter
RX=	*rmxon=*	Turn off XON/XOFF flow control (not in BSD 4.3).	13
sa=	*sgr=*	Set #1 #2 #3 #4 #5 #6 #7 #8 #9 attributes (mainly *terminfo*).	11
SA=	*smam=*	Turn on automatic margins (not in BSD 4.3).	10
sc=	*sc=*	Save absolute cursor position.	8
se=	*rmso=*	End standout mode.	11
sf=	*ind=*	Scroll forward one line.	8
SF=	*indn=*	Scroll forward #1 lines.	8
sg#	*xmc#*	Standout glitch: number of spaces printed when change to or from standout mode (default is 0).	11
sgr=	sa=	Set #1 #2 #3 #4 #5 #6 #7 #8 #9 attributes (mainly *terminfo*).	11
sgr0=	me=	Turn off all attributes.	11
smacs=	as=	Start using alternate character set.	11
smam=	SA=	Turn on automatic margins (not in BSD 4.3).	10
smcup=	ti=	Initialization for programs that use cursor motion.	10
smdc=	dm=	Begin delete mode.	9
smir=	im=	Begin insert mode.	9
smkx=	ks=	Turn keypad on, if can be turned on and off.	12
smln=	LO=	Turn soft labels on (not in BSD 4.3).	12
smm=	mm=	Meta mode on: put terminal into meta mode.	14
smso=	so=	Begin standout mode.	11
smul=	us=	Begin underline mode.	11
smxon=	SX=	Turn on XON/XOFF flow control (not in BSD 4.3).	13
so=	*smso=*	Begin standout mode.	11
sr=	*ri=*	Scroll reverse (backwards) one line.	8
SR=	*rin=*	Scroll reverse (backwards) #1 lines.	8
st=	*hts=*	Set a tab stop in all rows, current column.	10

Capa-bility	Equiv-alent	Description	Chap-ter
SX=	*smxon=*	Turn on XON/XOFF flow control (not in BSD 4.3).	13
ta=	*ht=*	Tab: move to next hardware tab stop (usually ^I).	10
tbc=	ct=	Clear all tab stops.	10
tc=	*use=*	Terminal copy: read terminal capabilities from a similar terminal.	15
te=	*rmcup=*	End programs that use cursor motion.	10
ti=	*smcup=*	Initialization for programs that use cursor motion.	10
ts=	*tsl=*	To status: send cursor to #1 column of status line.	8
tsl=	*ts=*	To status: send cursor to #1 column of status line.	8
uc=	*uc=*	Underline character at cursor, move cursor right.	11
UC	None	Upper case (obsolete).	16
ue=	*rmul=*	End underline mode.	11
ug#	None	Underline glitch: number of spaces printed when change to and from under-line mode. Only set if non-zero (not in *terminfo*). (See **xmc=**.)	11
ul	*ul*	Terminal underlines, even though it can-not overstrike.	11
up=	*cuu1=*	Move cursor up.	8
UP=	*cuu=*	Move cursor up a number of rows.	8
us=	*smul=*	Begin underline mode.	11
use=	tc=	Terminal copy: read terminal capabilities from a similar terminal.	15
vb=	*flash=*	Visual bell: flash terminal screen.	11
ve=	*cnorm=*	Make cursor normal (undo effect of **vs=** and **vi**).	11
vi=	*civis=*	Make cursor invisible.	11
vpa=	cv=	Move cursor vertically in its column to line #1.	8
vs=	*cvvis=*	Make cursor very visible.	11
vt#	*vt#*	Virtual terminal number (not supported on BSD systems).	16

Capability	Equivalent	Description	Chapter
wi=	*wind=*	Current window is lines #1 through #2, columns #3 through #4 (mainly *terminfo*).	16
wind=	wi=	Current window is lines #1 through #2, columns #3 through #4 (mainly *terminfo*).	16
ws#	*wsl#*	Specify width of status line if different from rest of screen.	8
wsl#	ws#	Specify width of status line if different from rest of screen.	8
xb	*xsb*	Beehive glitch (f1 key sends ESCAPE, f2 key sends ^C).	14
xenl	xn	Newline or wraparound glitch.	14
XF=	*xoffc=*	XOFF character: character to turn off input if not ^S (not in BSD 4.3).	13
xhp	xs	Standout glitch: text typed over standout text is automatically in standout mode.	14
xmc#	sg#	Standout glitch: number of spaces printed when change to or from standout mode (default is 0).	11
xn	*xenl*	Newline or wraparound glitch.	14
XN=	*xonc=*	XON character: character to turn on input, if not ^Q (not in BSD 4.3).	13
xo	*xon*	Terminal performs XON/XOFF flow control.	13
xoffc=	XF=	XOFF character: character to turn off input, if not ^S (not in BSD 4.3).	13
xon	xo	Terminal performs XON/XOFF flow control.	13
xonc=	XN=	XON character: character to turn on input, if not ^Q (not in BSD 4.3).	13
xr	None	Return glitch: return character clears the line (obsolete).	14
xs	*xhp*	Standout glitch: text typed over standout text is automatically in standout mode.	14
xsb	xb	Beehive glitch (f1 key sends ESCAPE, f2 key sends ^C).	14
xt	*xt*	Teleray glitch: has destructive tabs and odd standout mode.	14
xx	None	Tektronix 4025 line insert problem (obsolete).	14

Index

%3= capability 159
*3= capability 159
%4= capability 159
*4= capability 159
%5= capability 159
*5= capability 159
5i capability 174
%6= capability 159
*6= capability 159
%7= capability 159
*7= capability 159
%8= capability 159
*8= capability 159
%9= capability 159
*9= capability 159

A

%a= capability 159
absolute cursor movement, capa-
    bilities of 101
ac= capability 176
acsc= capability 176
adding to the screen, capabilities of
    112
ae= capability 139
AL= capability 112
al= capability 112
alias
  lines 31
  names 15
alternate character sets, capabilities
    of 139
am capability 18
am capability 184
argument encoding (see encoding
    run time arguments)
arrow keys 153
as= capability 139
at sign (@) 181
AT&T Toolchest 13

B

%b= capability 159
bc= capability 161
Beehive glitch 169
bel= capability 143
bells, capabilities of 143
Berkeley Software Distribution
    (see BSD)
bl= capability 143
blink= capability 139
bold= capability 139
Boolean capabilities
  5i 174
  am 18, 184
  am 184
  bs 17
  bs 107
  bw 184
  bw 184
  chts= 144
  conventions 92
  da 104
  da 104
  db 104
  db 104
  description of 16
  eo 184
  eo 184
  EP 189
  es 109
  eslok 109
  gn 28
  gn 184
  gn 184
  HC= 144
  HD= 189
  hs 109
  hs 109
  hz 168
  hz 168
  in 118
  in 118
  khome 153
  LC 189
  mc5i 174

K

kHOM= capability 159
khome capability 153
khts= capability 155
kI= capability 155
kichl= capability 155
kill= capability 155
kind= capability 155
kl= capability 153
kL= capability 155
klC= capability 159
kLFT= capability 159
kll= capability 155
kM= capability 155
kMOV= capability 159
kmov= capability 159
kmrk= capability 159
kMSG= capability 159
kmsg= capability 159
kn# capability 147
kN= capability 155
knp= capability 155
kNXT= capability 159
knxt= capability 159
ko= capability 155
kopn= capability 159
kopt= capability 159
kOT= capability 159
kP= capability 155
kpp= capability 155
kPRT= capability 159
kprt= capability 159
kprv= capability 159
kr= capability 153
kR= capability 155
kRDO= capability 159
krdo= capability 159
kref= capability 159
kRES= capability 159
kres= capability 159
krfr= capability 159
kri= capability 155
kRIT= capability 159
krmir capability 155
kRPL= capability 159

krpl= capability 159
krst= capability 159
ks= capability 153
kS= capability 155
kSAV= capability 159
ksav= capability 159
kslt= capability 159
kSPD= capability 159
kspd= capability 159
kT= capability 155
kt= capability 155
ktbc= capability 155
ku= capability 153
kUND= capability 159
kund= capability 159

L

l0= capability 147
l1= capability 147
l2= capability 147
l3= capability 147
l4= capability 147
l5= capability 147
l6= capability 147
l7= capability 147
l8= capability 147
l9= capability 147
la= capability 149
LC capability 189
-*lcurses* option 205
le= capability 97
LE= capability 100
LF= capability 161
lf0= capability 147
lf1= capability 147
lf10= capability 149
lf2= capability 147
lf3= capability 147
lf4= capability 147
lf5= capability 147
lf6= capability 147
lf7= capability 147

is2= 125		*kcudl*= 153	
is3= 125		*kcufl*= 153	
%j= 159		*kcuul*= 153	
k;= 149		kd= 153	
k= 159		kD= 155	
k0= 147		*kDC*= 159	
k1= 147		*kdchl*= 155	
K1= 153		*kdll*= 155	
k2= 147		ke= 153	
K2= 153		kE= 155	
k3= 147		*ked*= 155	
K3= 153		*kel*= 155	
k4= 147		*kEND*= 159	
K4= 153		*kend*= 159	
k5= 147		*kEOL*= 159	
K5= 153		*kEXT*= 159	
k6= 147		*kext*= 159	
k7= 147		kF= 155	
k8= 147		*kf0*= 147	
k9= 147		*kf1*= 147	
kA= 155		*kf10*= 149	
ka= 155		*kf11*= 149	
ka1= 153		*kf12*= 149	
ka3= 153		*kf13*= 149	
kB= 155		*kf19*= 149	
kb= 155		*kf2*= 147	
kb2= 153		*kf20*= 149	
kBEG= 159		*kf21*= 149	
kbeg= 159		*kf22*= 149	
kbs= 155		*kf3*= 147	
kC= 67, 155		*kf4*= 147	
kc1= 153		*kf44*= 149	
kc3= 153		*kf45*= 149	
kCAN= 159		*kf5*= 147	
kcan= 159		*kf6*= 147	
=*kcbt* 155		*kf7*= 147	
kclo= 159		*kf8*= 147	
kclr= 155		*kf9*= 147	
kCMD= 159		*kfind*= 159	
kcmd= 159		*kFND*= 159	
kCPY= 159		kh= 153	
kcpy= 159		kH= 155	
kCRT= 159		*khelp*= 159	
kcrt= 159		*kHLP*= 159	
kctab= 155		*kHOM*= 159	
kcubl= 153		*khts*= 155	

me= 139	*rmacs*= 139
mgc= 132	*rmam*= 132
mh= 139	*rmcup*= 127
mk= 139	*rmdc*= 114
ML= 132	*rmin*= 161
ml= 189	*rmir*= 118
mm= 178	*rmkx*= 153
mo= 178	*rmm*= 178
mp= 139	*rmp*= 163
MR= 132	*rmso*= 134
mr= 139	*rmxon*= 165
mrcup= 101	rp= 112
mu= 189	rP= 163
mul= 137	rs= 123
nd 18	*rs1*= 125
nd= 97	*rs2*= 125
nel= 107	*rs3*= 125
nl= 161	RX= 165
nw= 107	SA= 132
p0= 174	sa= 139, 142
pad= 163	sc= 101
pc= 163	*sc*= 101
pf= 174	se= 134
pfkey= 161	SF= 104
pfloc= 161	sf= 104
pfx= 161	*sgr*= 139
pin= 161	*sgr0*= 139
pk= 161	*smacs*= 139
pl= 161	*smam*= 132
pn= 161	*smcup*= 127
po= 174	*smdc*= 114
prot= 139	*smgl*= 132
ps= 174	*smin*= 161
px= 161	*smir*= 118
RA= 132	*smkx*= 153
rc= 101	*smm*= 178
rc= 101	*smrg*= 132
rep= 112	*smso*= 134
rev= 139	*smul*= 137
rf= 123	*smxon*= 165
rf= 125	so= 134
RF= 184	SR= 104
rfi 184	sr= 104
RI= 100	st= 129
ri= 104	SX= 165
rin= 104	ta= 129

About the Authors

Linda Mui is an employee of O'Reilly & Associates. At ORA she has worked in system administration and user support, specializing in UNIX text processing tools. Linda also co-authored the *X Window System Administrator Guide*. Linda was born and raised in New York City. She currently lives in Cambridge, MA. Her summer hobbies are lazing on her hammock, taking long aimless drives, and attempting to play tennis. Her winter hobbies are reading, cooking, and waiting for summer.

Tim O'Reilly is founder and president of O'Reilly & Associates, publisher of the X Window System series and the popular Nutshell Handbooks on UNIX. Tim has written or edited many of the books published by ORA. He is also the author of a book about science fiction writer Frank Herbert. Tim's long-term vision for the company is to create a vehicle for creative people to support themselves by exploring interesting ideas. Technical book publishing is just the first step. Tim graduated cum laude from Harvard in 1975 with a B.A. in Classics.

Colophon

Our look is the result of reader comments, our own experimentation, and distribution channels. Distinctive covers complement our distinctive approach to UNIX documentation, breathing personality and life into potentially dry subjects. UNIX and its attendant programs can be unruly beasts. Nutshell Handbooks help you tame them.

The animal featured on the cover of *termcap and terminfo* is a great black cockatoo. This large crested parrot is native to Australia and islands in the Malayan Archipelago. Largest of all the parrots, the great black cockatoo can grow up to 32 inches in height. It has bluish-black plumage with bare, pink cheeks that redden when it becomes excited. As a cockatoo, it is distinguished from other parrots in its ability to raise the feathers of its crest.

Edie Freedman designed this cover and the entire UNIX bestiary that appears on other Nutshell Handbooks. The beasts themselves are adapted from 19th-century engravings from the Dover Pictorial Archive.

The text of this book is set in Times Roman; headings are Helvetica; examples are Courier. Text was prepared using SoftQuad's *sqtroff* text formatter. Printing is done on an Apple LaserWriter. Whenever possible, our books use RepKover™, a durable and flexible lay-flat binding. If the page count exceeds RepKover's limit, perfect binding is used.

More Titles from O'Reilly

System Administration

Managing NFS and NIS

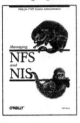

By Hal Stern
1st Edition June 1991
436 pages, ISBN 0-937175-75-7

Managing NFS and NIS is for system administrators who need to set up or manage a network filesystem installation. NFS (Network Filesystem) is probably running at any site that has two or more UNIX systems. NIS (Network Information System) is a distributed database used to manage a network of computers. The only practical book devoted entirely to these subjects, this guide is a "must-have" for anyone interested in UNIX networking.

Essential System Administration

By Æleen Frisch
2nd Edition September 1995
788 pages, ISBN 1-56592-127-5

Thoroughly revised and updated for all major versions of UNIX, this second edition of Essential System Administration provides a compact, manageable introduction to the tasks faced by everyone responsible for a UNIX system. Whether you use a stand-alone UNIX system, routinely provide administrative support for a larger shared system, or just want an understanding of basic administrative functions, this book is for you. Offers expanded sections on networking, electronic mail, security, and kernel configuration.

Volume 8: X Window System Administrator's Guide

By Linda Mui & Eric Pearce
1st Edition October 1992
372 pages, ISBN 0-937175-83-8

This book focuses on issues of system administration for X and X-based networks—not just for UNIX system administrators, but for anyone faced with the job of administering X (including those running X on stand-alone workstations).

Using Samba

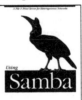

By Peter Kelly, Perry Donham & David Collier-Brown
1st Edition April 1999 (est.)
300 pages (est.),
Includes CD-ROM
ISBN 1-56592-449-5

Samba turns a UNIX or Linux system into a file and print server for Microsoft Windows network clients. This complete guide to Samba administration covers basic 2.0 configuration, security, logging, and troubleshooting. Whether you're playing on one note or a full three-octave range, this book will help you maintain an efficient and secure server. Includes a CD-ROM of sources and ready-to-install binaries.

System Performance Tuning

By Mike Loukides
1st Edition November 1990
336 pages, ISBN 0-937175-60-9

System Performance Tuning answers the fundamental question: How can I get my UNIX-based computer to do more work without buying more hardware? Some performance problems do require you to buy a bigger or faster computer, but many can be solved simply by making better use of the resources you already have.

O'REILLY®

TO ORDER: **800-998-9938** • *order@oreilly.com* • *http://www.oreilly.com/*
OUR PRODUCTS ARE AVAILABLE AT A BOOKSTORE OR SOFTWARE STORE NEAR YOU.
FOR INFORMATION: **800-998-9938** • **707-829-0515** • *info@oreilly.com*

UNIX Basics

Learning the Korn Shell

By Bill Rosenblatt
1st Edition June 1993
360 pages, ISBN 1-56592-054-6

A thorough introduction to
the Korn shell, both as a user
interface and as a programming
language. This book provides a
clear explanation of the Korn
shell's features, including *ksh*
string operations, co-processes, signals and signal
handling, and command-line interpretation. *Learning
the Korn Shell* also includes real-life programming
examples and a Korn shell debugger (*kshdb*).

Using csh and tcsh

By Paul DuBois
1st Edition August 1995
242 pages, ISBN 1-56592-132-1

Using csh and tcsh describes
from the beginning how to use
these shells interactively to get
your work done faster with less
typing. You'll learn how to make
your prompt tell you where
you are (no more pwd); use what you've typed before
(history); type long command lines with few keystrokes
(command and filename completion); remind yourself
of filenames when in the middle of typing a command;
and edit a botched command without retyping it.

Learning the vi Editor, 6th Edition

By Linda Lamb & Arnold Robbins
6th Edition October 1998
348 pages, ISBN 1-56592-426-6

This completely updated guide
to editing with vi, the editor
available on nearly every
UNIX system, now covers four
popular vi clones and includes
command summaries for
easy reference. It starts with the basics, followed by
more advanced editing tools, such as ex commands,
global search and replacement, and a new feature,
multi-screen editing.

Learning the UNIX Operating System, 4th Edition

By Jerry Peek, Grace Todino &
John Strang
4th Edition December 1997
106 pages, ISBN 1-56592-390-1

If you are new to UNIX, this concise
introduction will tell you just what
you need to get started and no
more. The new fourth edition
covers the Linux operating system
and is an ideal primer for someone
just starting with UNIX or Linux, as well as for Mac and PC
users who encounter a UNIX system on the Internet. This
classic book, still the most effective introduction to UNIX
in print, now includes a quick-reference card.

Learning GNU Emacs, 2nd Edition

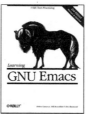

By Debra Cameron,
Bill Rosenblatt & Eric Raymond
2nd Edition September 1996
560 pages, ISBN 1-56592-152-6

Learning GNU Emacs is an
introduction to Version 19.30
of the GNU Emacs editor, one
of the most widely used and
powerful editors available
under UNIX. It provides a solid
introduction to basic editing, a look at several important
"editing modes" (special Emacs features for editing
specific types of documents, including email, Usenet
News, and the World Wide Web), and a brief introduction
to customization and Emacs LISP programming. The
book is aimed at new Emacs users, whether or not they
are programmers. Includes quick-reference card.

UNIX Basics

Volume 3M: X Window System User's Guide, Motif Edition, 2nd Edition

By Valerie Quercia & Tim O'Reilly
2nd Edition January 1993
956 pages, ISBN 1-56592-015-5

The *X Window System User's Guide, Motif Edition* orients the new user to window system concepts and provides detailed tutorials for many client programs, including the xtermterminal emulator and the twm, uwm, and mwmwindow managers. Later chapters explain how to customize the X environment. Revised for Motif 1.2 and X11 Release 5.

UNIX Tools

Applying RCS and SCCS

By Don Bolinger & Tan Bronson
1st Edition September 1995
528 pages, ISBN 1-56592-117-8

Applying RCS and SCCS is a thorough introduction to these two systems, viewed as tools for project management. This book takes the reader from basic source control of a single file, through working with multiple releases of a software project, to coordinating multiple developers. It also presents TCCS, a representative "front-end" that addresses problems RCS and SCCS can't handle alone, such as managing groups of files, developing for multiple platforms, and linking public and private development areas.

UNIX Tools

Managing Projects with make, 2nd Edition

By Andrew Oram & Steve Talbott
2nd Edition October 1991
152 pages, ISBN 0-937175-90-0

make is one of UNIX's greatest contributions to software development, and this book is the clearest description of make ever written. It describes all the basic features of make and provides guidelines on meeting the needs of large, modern projects. Also contains a description of free products that contain major enhancements to make.

UNIX Power Tools, 2nd Edition

By Jerry Peek, Tim O'Reilly & Mike Loukides
2nd Edition August 1997
1120 pages, Includes CD-ROM
ISBN 1-56592-260-3

Loaded with even more practical advice about almost every aspect of UNIX, this new second edition of *UNIX Power Tools* addresses the technology that UNIX users face today. You'll find increased coverage of POSIX utilities, including GNU versions, greater *bash* and *tcsh* shell coverage, more emphasis on Perl, and a CD-ROM that contains the best freeware available.

Writing GNU Emacs Extensions

By Bob Glickstein
1st Edition April 1997
236 pages, ISBN 1-56592-261-1

This book introduces Emacs Lisp and tells you how to make the editor do whatever you want, whether it's altering the way text scrolls or inventing a whole new "major mode." Topics progress from simple to complex, from lists, symbols, and keyboard commands to syntax tables, macro templates, and error recovery.

O'REILLY®

TO ORDER: **800-998-9938** • **order@oreilly.com** • **http://www.oreilly.com/**
OUR PRODUCTS ARE AVAILABLE AT A BOOKSTORE OR SOFTWARE STORE NEAR YOU.
FOR INFORMATION: **800-998-9938** • **707-829-0515** • **info@oreilly.com**

UNIX Tools

Exploring Expect

By Don Libes
1st Edition December 1994
602 pages, ISBN 1-56592-090-2

Written by the author of Expect, this is the first book to explain how this part of the UNIX tool-box can be used to automate Telnet, FTP, passwd, rlogin, and hundreds of other interactive applications. Based on Tcl (Tool Command Language), Expect lets you automate interactive applications that have previously been extremely difficult to handle with any scripting language.

The UNIX CD Bookshelf

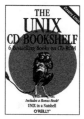

By O'Reilly & Associates, Inc.
1st Edition November 1998
444 pages
Includes CD-ROM & book
ISBN 1-56592-406-1

The UNIX CD Bookshelf contains six books from O'Reilly plus the software from UNIX Power Tools —all on a convenient CD-ROM. A bonus hardcopy book, *UNIX in a Nutshell: System V Edition*, is also included. The CD-ROM contains *UNIX in a Nutshell: System V Edition*; *UNIX Power Tools, 2nd Edition* (with software); *Learning the UNIX Operating System, 4th Edition*; *Learning the vi Editor, 6th Edition*; *sed & awk, 2nd Edition*; and *Learning the Korn Shell*.

Tcl/Tk Tools

By Mark Harrison
1st Edition September 1997
678 pages, Includes CD-ROM
ISBN 1-56592-218-2

One of the greatest strengths of Tcl/Tk is the range of extensions written for it. This book clearly documents the most popular and robust extensions—by the people who created them—and contains information on configuration, debugging, and other important tasks. The CD-ROM includes Tcl/Tk, the extensions, and other tools documented in the text both in source form and as binaries for Solaris and Linux.

Software Portability with imake, 2nd Edition

By Paul DuBois
2nd Edition September 1996
410 pages, ISBN 1-56592-226-3

This Nutshell Handbook®—the only book available on *imake*— is ideal for X and UNIX program-mers who want their software to be portable. The second edition covers the current version of the X Window System (X11R6.1), using *imake* for non-UNIX systems such as Windows NT, and some of the quirks about using *imake* under OpenWindows/ Solaris.

UNIX Tools

Programming with GNU Software

By Mike Loukides & Andy Oram
1st Edition December 1996
260 pages, ISBN 1-56592-112-7

This book and CD combination is a complete package for programmers who are new to UNIX or who would like to make better use of the system. The tools come from Cygnus Support, Inc., and Cyclic Software, companies that provide support for free software. Contents include GNU Emacs, *gcc*, C and C++ libraries, *gdb*, RCS, and *make*. The book provides an introduction to all these tools for a C programmer.

Tcl/Tk in a Nutshell

By Paul Raines & Jeff Tranter
1st Edition January 1999 (est.)
480 pages, ISBN 1-56592-433-9

The Tcl language and Tk graphical toolkit are powerful building blocks for applications that feature a variety of commands with a wealth of options in each command. This quick reference briefly describes every command and option in the core Tcl/Tk distribution, as well as the most popular extensions. Keep it on your desk as you write scripts, and you'll be able to quickly find the particular option you need.

lex & yacc, 2nd Edition

By John Levine, Tony Mason & Doug Brown
2nd Edition October 1992
366 pages, ISBN 1-56592-000-7

This book shows programmers how to use two UNIX utilities, lex and yacc, in program development. The second edition contains completely revised tutorial sections for novice users and reference sections for advanced users. This edition is twice the size of the first, has an expanded index, and covers Bison and Flex.

sed & awk, 2nd Edition

By Dale Dougherty & Arnold Robbins
2nd Edition March 1997
432 pages, ISBN 1-56592-225-5

sed & awk describes two text manipulation programs that are mainstays of the UNIX programmer's toolbox. This new edition covers the *sed* and *awk* programs as they are now mandated by the POSIX standard and includes discussion of the GNU versions of these programs.

O'REILLY®

TO ORDER: **800-998-9938** • **order@oreilly.com** • **http://www.oreilly.com/**
OUR PRODUCTS ARE AVAILABLE AT A BOOKSTORE OR SOFTWARE STORE NEAR YOU.
FOR INFORMATION: **800-998-9938** • **707-829-0515** • **info@oreilly.com**

How to stay in touch with O'Reilly

1. Visit Our Award-Winning Site

http://www.oreilly.com/

★ "Top 100 Sites on the Web" —*PC Magazine*
★ "Top 5% Web sites" —*Point Communications*
★ "3-Star site" —*The McKinley Group*

Our web site contains a library of comprehensive product information (including book excerpts and tables of contents), downloadable software, background articles, interviews with technology leaders, links to relevant sites, book cover art, and more. File us in your Bookmarks or Hotlist!

2. Join Our Email Mailing Lists

New Product Releases

To receive automatic email with brief descriptions of all new O'Reilly products as they are released, send email to:
listproc@online.oreilly.com
Put the following information in the first line of your message (*not* in the Subject field):
subscribe oreilly-news

O'Reilly Events

If you'd also like us to send information about trade show events, special promotions, and other O'Reilly events, send email to:
listproc@online.oreilly.com
Put the following information in the first line of your message (*not* in the Subject field):
subscribe oreilly-events

3. Get Examples from Our Books via FTP

There are two ways to access an archive of example files from our books:

Regular FTP

* ftp to:
ftp.oreilly.com
(login: anonymous
password: your email address)
* Point your web browser to:
ftp://ftp.oreilly.com/

FTPMAIL

* Send an email message to:
ftpmail@online.oreilly.com
(Write "help" in the message body)

4. Contact Us via Email

order@oreilly.com
To place a book or software order online. Good for North American and international customers.

subscriptions@oreilly.com
To place an order for any of our newsletters or periodicals.

books@oreilly.com
General questions about any of our books.

software@oreilly.com
For general questions and product information about our software. Check out O'Reilly Software Online at **http://software.oreilly.com/** for software and technical support information. Registered O'Reilly software users send your questions to: **website-support@oreilly.com**

cs@oreilly.com
For answers to problems regarding your order or our products.

booktech@oreilly.com
For book content technical questions or corrections.

proposals@oreilly.com
To submit new book or software proposals to our editors and product managers.

international@oreilly.com
For information about our international distributors or translation queries. For a list of our distributors outside of North America check out:
http://www.oreilly.com/www/order/country.html

O'Reilly & Associates, Inc.
101 Morris Street, Sebastopol, CA 95472 USA
TEL   707-829-0515 or 800-998-9938
       (6am to 5pm PST)
FAX   707-829-0104

O'REILLY®

TO ORDER: **800-998-9938** • **order@oreilly.com** • **http://www.oreilly.com/**
OUR PRODUCTS ARE AVAILABLE AT A BOOKSTORE OR SOFTWARE STORE NEAR YOU.
FOR INFORMATION: **800-998-9938** • **707-829-0515** • **info@oreilly.com**

International Distributors

UK, EUROPE, MIDDLE EAST AND NORTHERN AFRICA (EXCEPT FRANCE, GERMANY, SWITZERLAND, & AUSTRIA)

INQUIRIES
International Thomson Publishing Europe
Berkshire House
168-173 High Holborn
London WC1V 7AA, United Kingdom
Telephone: 44-171-497-1422
Fax: 44-171-497-1426
Email: itpint@itps.co.uk

ORDERS
International Thomson Publishing
Services, Ltd.
Cheriton House, North Way
Andover, Hampshire SP10 5BE
United Kingdom
Telephone: 44-264-342-832 (UK)
Telephone: 44-264-342-806 (outside UK)
Fax: 44-264-364418 (UK)
Fax: 44-264-342761 (outside UK)
UK & Eire orders: itpuk@itps.co.uk
International orders: itpint@itps.co.uk

FRANCE
Editions Eyrolles
61 bd Saint-Germain
75240 Paris Cedex 05, France
Fax: 33-01-44-41-11-44

FRENCH LANGUAGE BOOKS
All countries except Canada
Telephone: 33-01-44-41-46-16
Email: geodif@eyrolles.com
English language books
Telephone: 33-01-44-41-11-87
Email: distribution@eyrolles.com

GERMANY, SWITZERLAND, AND AUSTRIA

INQUIRIES
O'Reilly Verlag
Balthasarstr. 81
D-50670 Köln, Germany
Telephone: 49-221-97-31-60-0
Fax: 49-221-97-31-60-8
Email: anfragen@oreilly.de

ORDERS
International Thomson Publishing
Königswinterer Straße 418
53227 Bonn, Germany
Telephone: 49-228-97024 0
Fax: 49-228-441342
Email: order@oreilly.de

JAPAN
O'Reilly Japan, Inc.
Kiyoshige Building 2F
12-Banchi, Sanei-cho
Shinjuku-ku
Tokyo 160-0008 Japan
Telephone: 81-3-3356-5227
Fax: 81-3-3356-5261
Email: kenji@oreilly.com

INDIA
Computer Bookshop (India) PVT. LTD.
190 Dr. D.N. Road, Fort
Bombay 400 001 India
Telephone: 91-22-207-0989
Fax: 91-22-262-3551
Email: cbsbom@giasbm01.vsnl.net.in

HONG KONG
City Discount Subscription Service Ltd.
Unit D, 3rd Floor, Yan's Tower
27 Wong Chuk Hang Road
Aberdeen, Hong Kong
Telephone: 852-2580-3539
Fax: 852-2580-6463
Email: citydis@ppn.com.hk

KOREA
Hanbit Media, Inc.
Sonyoung Bldg. 202
Yeksam-dong 736-36
Kangnam-ku
Seoul, Korea
Telephone: 822-554-9610
Fax: 822-556-0363
Email: hant93@chollian.dacom.co.kr

SINGAPORE, MALAYSIA, THAILAND
Addison Wesley Longman Singapore
PTE Ltd.
25 First Lok Yang Road
Singapore 629734
Telephone: 65-268-2666
Fax: 65-268-7023
Email: daniel@longman.com.sg

PHILIPPINES
Mutual Books, Inc.
429-D Shaw Boulevard
Mandaluyong City, Metro
Manila, Philippines
Telephone: 632-725-7538
Fax: 632-721-3056
Email: mbikikog@mnl.sequel.net

CHINA
Ron's DataCom Co., Ltd.
79 Dongwu Avenue
Dongxihu District
Wuhan 430040
China
Telephone: 86-27-3892568
Fax: 86-27-3222108
Email: hongfeng@public.wh.hb.cn

ALL OTHER ASIAN COUNTRIES
O'Reilly & Associates, Inc.
101 Morris Street
Sebastopol, CA 95472 USA
Telephone: 707-829-0515
Fax: 707-829-0104
Email: order@oreilly.com

AUSTRALIA
WoodsLane Pty. Ltd.
7/5 Vuko Place, Warriewood NSW 2102
P.O. Box 935
Mona Vale NSW 2103
Australia
Telephone: 61-2-9970-5111
Fax: 61-2-9970-5002
Email: info@woodslane.com.au

NEW ZEALAND
Woodslane New Zealand Ltd.
21 Cooks Street (P.O. Box 575)
Waganui, New Zealand
Telephone: 64-6-347-6543
Fax: 64-6-345-4840
Email: info@woodslane.com.au

THE AMERICAS
McGraw-Hill Interamericana Editores,
S.A. de C.V.
Cedro No. 512
Col. Atlampa 06450
Mexico, D.F.
Telephone: 52-5-541-3155
Fax: 52-5-541-4913
Email: mcgraw-hill@infosel.net.mx

SOUTH AFRICA
International Thomson Publishing
South Africa
Building 18, Constantia Park
138 Sixteenth Road
P.O. Box 2459
Halfway House, 1685 South Africa
Telephone: 27-11-805-4819
Fax: 27-11-805-3648